Blasphemy

BOOKS BY ALAN DERSHOWITZ

Blasphemy

How the Religious Right Is Hijacking
Our Declaration of Independence

Alan Dershowitz

BICENTENNIAL
1807
WILEY
2007
BICENTENNIAL

John Wiley & Sons, Inc.

To my great nephew Mars
"Question with boldness."
—Thomas Jefferson to his nephew

CONTENTS

ACKNOWLEDGMENTS

Skepticism and open-mindedness are what I value most in my student research assistants. Those who helped me on this book combine those Jeffersonian traits with intelligence, creativity, and responsibility. Thanks, therefore, go to Alex Blenkinsopp, Charles Johnson, and Chaim Kagedan. Thanks as well to Eric Citron, who helped me with the historical research for *America Declares Independence*, from which some of the material in this volume is adapted. Thanks also to Nichele McClendon for typing the manuscript, and to friends and family members who critiqued it. My appreciation also goes to the folks at Wiley, especially my editor, Hana Lane, and to my literary agent, Helen Rees. Any blasphemous statements contained in this book are, however, my responsibility alone.

INTRODUCTION

Is the United States a Christian Nation?

The Religious Right is engaged in a crusade to convert the United States into a Christian theocracy based on the Bible and, more specifically, on the divine authority of Jesus Christ. This is not the first time in history that religious fundamentalism has sought to declare our heterogeneous country to be a "Christian nation," but all previous efforts in this direction have been rejected. This time a new tactic is being used, and it promises—or threatens—a greater potential for success. In an appeal to the founding fathers, the Religious Right is employing as their primary weapon the Declaration of Independence, which they claim is America's baptismal certificate. They point to the words of the Declaration—its invocation of "Nature's God," "Creator," "Supreme Judge of the World," and "Divine Providence"—as proof that our nation was founded on the principles of Christianity, Jesus Christ, and the Holy Bible. They also seek to elevate the Declaration of

1

Independence to equal legal status with the Constitution, which contains no references to God and prohibits any religious test for federal office and any law respecting an establishment of religion. As David Barton, an advocate of a Christianized America, has put it: "Many people erroneously consider the Constitution to be a higher document than the Declaration. However, under our form of government, the Constitution is *not* superior to the Declaration of Independence; a violation of the Declaration is just as serious as a breach of the Constitution" (emphasis in original).[1] Barton further argues that "[t]he Constitution cannot be properly interpreted or applied apart from the natural law principles presented in the Declaration. The two documents must be used together to understand either one individually."[2] This view of the legal status of the Declaration has never been accepted by the courts, but it is regarded as gospel by many on the Religious Right.

Invoking the beliefs of the founders, and especially the Declaration of Independence, is a powerful weapon indeed. As Jon Meacham, the author of *American Gospel*, has written:

> The intensity with which the Religious Right attempts to conscript the Founders into their cause indicates the importance the movement ascribes to historical benediction by association with the origins of the Republic. If [they] convince enough people that America was a Christian nation that has lost its way, the more legitimate their efforts in the political arena seem.[3]

The *Washington Post* columnist George F. Will has put it more bluntly:

> Not since the medieval church baptized, as it were, Aristotle, as some sort of early—very early—church father

has there been an intellectual hijacking as audacious as the attempt to present America's principal founders as devout Christians. Such an attempt is now in high gear among people who argue that the founders were kindred spirits with today's evangelicals, and that they founded a "Christian nation."[4]

Many on the Religious Right are sincere and decent people who deeply believe they are doing God's work. And maybe they are, but they are not doing Jefferson's work, or the work of our other founders who strongly believed in the separation of church and state. The good people who are using the Declaration of Independence to Christianize our nation have a very different conception of governance from that of the founding generation, and it is wrong for these historical revisionists to rewrite our past in an effort to change our future.

In this book I will revisit the history of our Declaration and the philosophy of its drafters in an effort to reclaim this foundational document for all Americans, not just those who adhere to one particular belief system.

American independence from Great Britain was achieved on the battlefield, but the establishment of a new republic, conceived in liberty, was as much a product of the pen as the sword. As Thomas Paine, whose own pen contributed to the willingness of colonial Americans to take up the sword—and who, in January 1776, called for a "declaration of Independence"—wrote several years after the American Revolution: "[T]he independence of America, considered merely as a separation from England, would have been a matter of but little importance." It became an event worthy of celebration because it was "accompanied by a revolution in the principles and practice of governments."[5]

This book is about the revolution in principles wrought by

the pens of American statesmen, rather than the revolution won by the swords and flintlocks of American patriots. Although it is difficult, as a historical matter, to separate words from deeds, my focus will be on the words and ideas used to justify the revolution, and their enduring impact on the "Course of human Events," most particularly the rights of men and women throughout the world.

I have always been intrigued by the Declaration of Independence. Though an important document of liberty, it is a hodgepodge of political, religious, and historical theories. It invokes the laws of nature, as if nature speaks with a single moral voice, and the law of nature's silent God, rather than Christianity's God of revelation. It describes rights as "unalienable" and declares that "all Men are created equal," and yet it presupposes the continued enslavement of men, women, and children who were certainly being denied the unalienable right to liberty "endowed" to them by their Creator. From these natural and God-given rights, the Declaration shifts effortlessly to social contract theory, declaring that governments derive "their just Powers from the Consent of the Governed" rather than from some natural or divine law.

The document then moves to a series of alleged wrongs committed against the colonists by the king. Some are profound, such as rendering the military superior to the civil power and denying the benefits of a trial by jury. Some seem trivial, even whiny, such as creating new offices "to harrass our People, and eat out their Substance." Yet other descriptions of wrongs are shameful in their overt racism, such as the reference to "the merciless Indian Savages, whose known Rule of Warfare, is an undistinguished Destruction, of all Ages, Sexes and Conditions."

Finally, the Declaration invokes the claim of "necessity," then proclaims "a firm Reliance on the Protection of Divine Providence" and pledges the lives, fortunes, and sacred honor of the signers to the cause of independence.

In light of this oft-conflicting rhetoric, it should come as no surprise that its words have been wrenched out of context by partisan pleaders to promote parochial causes. Natural law advocates point to the "Laws of Nature." Libertarians focus on the claim of unalienable rights, especially that of "Liberty." Most recently those who would break down the wall of separation between church and state try to use Thomas Jefferson's own words as battering rams against the structure he himself helped to build. Despite the fact that the Declaration expressly eschewed any mention of the Bible—since some of the most influential of our founding fathers were deists who did not believe in the divine origin of the Bible—modern-day advocates cite the Declaration's invocation of "Nature's God" and "Creator" as proof that we are a Christian or a Judeo-Christian nation founded on Scripture.

In the pages to come, I will examine the various intellectual, religious, and political currents that run through this complex and often misused document of liberty and explore its appropriate place in our structure of government.

This book seeks to reclaim the Declaration for all Americans—indeed, for all people who love liberty and abhor tyranny both of the body and the mind. A review of the history, theology, and political theory underlying the Declaration of Independence will demonstrate that its purpose was not only to provide a justification for our separation from England but also to provide a foundation for a new kind of polity based on "the Consent of the Governed" and, as Jefferson later wrote, the "unbound exercise of reason and freedom of opinion." The Declaration itself was as revolutionary as the course of conduct it sought to justify to "the Opinions of Mankind." Yet we must exercise considerable caution in extrapolating the words of the past to the issues of the present. As I will try to show, the very meanings of words and concepts change markedly with the times. As Oliver Wendell Holmes Jr. wisely observed, "a word is not a crystal, transparent and unchanged; it is the skin of a living thought and may vary greatly in color and context according to the circumstances and time in which it is used."[6] Even words as apparently timeless as "God," "nature," "equal," and "rights" convey somewhat different meanings today from what they did in 1776.

But first, a brief word about the actual revolution that was the particular subject of the Declaration will place that document in its historical, political, and military setting. The Declaration of Independence, as we all know, was approved on July 4, 1776, but the struggle for independence began well before that iconic date and was to continue for some time thereafter. Historians disagree as to the specific event that marked the beginning of our revolution, since there was no formal declaration of war or any other specific signpost on the long road to separation. Some go back as far as the Boston Massacre of 1770, while others point to the Boston Tea Party in 1773. Most focus on the first actual battle between British soldiers and American patriots, at Lexington and Concord in 1775, where "the shot heard round the world" was fired. The reality is that, as with most complex historical epics, there was no singular event that marked its commencement. The American Revolution was an ongoing process, as the British would surely have argued had they won the war and placed our revolutionaries—from Samuel Adams to James Madison—in the dock for treason.

Among the most prominent defendants would have been those courageous men who evaded British arrest and made it to Philadelphia to attend the First and Second Continental Congresses, in 1775 and 1776. The actual resolution by which the Continental Congress officially voted to separate from Great Britain—the primary overt act of treason—was submitted on June 7, 1776, by Richard Henry Lee (hardly a household name) and was approved on July 2, 1776 (hardly a memorable date). It was an eminently forgettable bare-bones resolution that simply affirmed what everyone already knew to be the fact: that, as Thomas Paine had correctly observed, the period of debate was over and the time had come to declare that "these United Colonies are, and of Right ought to be, Free Independent States, that they are absolved from all Allegiance to the British Crown, and that all political connection between them and the State of Great-Britain is and ought to be totally dissolved."[7]

The Declaration of Independence, approved two days later, was, essentially, an explanation of and justification for the action already taken. It was analogous to a judicial opinion delivered several days after the actual judgment had been rendered by a court.

The Continental Congress decided on this bifurcated approach in early June 1776, when, following the introduction of Lee's resolution, it appointed a committee to "prepare a declaration to the effect of the said first resolution." Thomas Jefferson, John Adams, Benjamin Franklin, Roger Sherman, and Robert Livingston were appointed to serve on the committee. There is some disagreement as to how Jefferson came to draft the Declaration. Adams recalled that Jefferson had proposed that the two of them jointly produce a first draft, but that he deferred to Jefferson because the younger man was a better writer—"you can write ten times better than I can"[8]—and a Virginian. Adams also believed that he himself was "obnoxious, suspected, and unpopular," while Jefferson was "very much otherwise."[9] Jefferson remembered it differently. The committee simply chose him to draft the Declaration: "I consented: I drew it [up]."[10]

There is no disagreement about the fact that Jefferson did compose the first draft and that most of the words of the final document—including its most memorable ones—were his. In his biography of John Adams, David McCullough described the drafting process:

> Alone in his upstairs parlor at Seventh and Market, Jefferson went to work, seated in an unusual revolving Windsor chair and holding on his lap a portable writing box, a small folding desk of his own design which, like the chair, he had specially made for him by a Philadelphia cabinetmaker. Traffic rattled by below the open windows. The June days and nights turned increasingly warm. He worked rapidly and, to judge by surviving drafts, with a sure command of his material. He had none of his books with him, or needed any he later claimed. It was not his objective to be original, he would explain, only to "place before mankind the common sense of the subject."[11]

In Jefferson's own view, his draft of the Declaration neither aimed at "originality of principle or sentiment, nor yet copied from any particular and previous writing, it was intended to be an expression of the American mind, and to give to that expression the proper tone and spirit called for by the occasion."[12]

While Jefferson was busily writing the words that would help define our new nation—if it were to prevail on the battlefield—George Washington was receiving word that a British fleet of 132 vessels had sailed from Canada and was expected to attack New York. Another 53 warships were approaching Charleston, South Carolina. The most powerful armada and the greatest army ever to reach this continent were poised to attack our cities and seaports. As the historian Joseph J. Ellis reminds us, the members of the Continental Congress were "preoccupied with more pressing military and strategic considerations in the summer of 1776 and did not regard the drafting of the Declaration as their highest priority."[13] But for the man assigned to draft it, nothing could be more important.

Jefferson understood that the immediate purpose of the Declaration was to aid the war effort, both by rallying the troops and in soliciting the support of potential allies. But he had a longer view of the Declaration's ultimate purpose. In an 1826 letter he wrote to the chairman of the fiftieth anniversary celebration of American independence just days before his own death, Jefferson explained that he intended the words of the Declaration to be "to the world . . . the signal of arousing men to burst the chains under which monkish ignorance and superstition had persuaded them to bind themselves, and to assume the blessings and security of self-government."[14] In the ensuing chapters we will try to understand what Jefferson, and those who edited and ratified his draft, meant by these ambitious ideas. We will also see how difficult it is to invoke words written at one point in history as definitive guides to the resolution of issues that divide a very different people at a very different time, and yet how important it is to remain inspired by the revolutionary spirit that animated these powerful words and ideas.[15]

1

The God of the Declaration

Is He the God of Today's Christian Right?

I would see no constitutional problem if schoolchildren were taught the nature of the Founding Fathers' religious beliefs and how these beliefs affected the attitudes of the times and the structure of our government.

—Justice Lewis Powell[1]

The Declaration of Independence has been called the birth certificate of America. In recent years, however, partisans of the Religious Right have tried to transmogrify this document of liberty into a baptismal certificate for a Christianized America. They point to its invocation of God to support their sectarian reading of the Declaration.

It is, of course, true that the Declaration proclaims that "the Laws of Nature and of *Nature's God*" entitle the American people to separate and equal station with their mother country. It also postulates as a self-evident truth that "all Men

11

are created equal [and] are endowed *by their Creator* with certain unalienable Rights" and then appeals to "the *Supreme Judge* of the World." Finally, it expresses "a firm Reliance on the Protection of *Divine Providence*." (Emphases added in these passages.) It is these references to "Nature's God," "Creator," "Supreme Judge," and "Divine Providence" that have been cited as proof of our founding fathers' commitment to the Judeo-Christian God of the Bible.

But these were terms—especially "Nature's God"— "employed not by conventional Christians but by Enlightenment 'deists.'"[2] The omission of any reference to Jesus Christ, or to the specific God of Christianity or of the Bible is far more significant than the inclusion of generic words that were consistent with non-Christian deistic beliefs.

As I will show in the pages to come, the Declaration was not based on the Bible, and its drafters were most definitely not "men of the Bible." On the contrary, Thomas Jefferson, its primary drafter, believed that the New Testament was written largely by "very inferior minds"[3] and that much of it consisted of "so much absurdity, so much untruth, charlatanism and imposture"[4] that it could aptly be characterized as "dung."[5] He thought even less of the Old Testament, whose vengeful God he deplored and whose draconian laws he rejected. He did not believe that the Ten Commandments, with their inclusion of punishment of children for the sins of their fathers, came from God, and he characterized the history of the Old Testament as "defective" and "doubtful." As for the supposed miracles of the Bible, he compared them to the false miracles of Greek and Roman mythology. He rejected the "supernatural" and regarded the concept of the Trinity as "insane." He specifically disagreed with Blackstone's claim that "the Law of Moses" was the basis of English law, characterizing this claim as a "fraud" based on an "awkward monkish fabrication."[6] He even wrote a disquisition against the judicial "usurpation" that sought to base English governance on "laws made for the Jews alone, and the precepts of the gospel."[7]

Thomas Jefferson was neither a man of the Bible nor a person "of faith." He was a man of science and reason. Jefferson abhorred St. Augustine's curse against "the one that trusteth in Man,"[8] for he was one who placed his trust in human reason over biblical revelation. He rejected the traditional Christian belief that all men were fallen sinners, and he despised the notion of God having chosen certain peoples for favorable or unfavorable treatment.

It is difficult to imagine a man less of the Bible than Thomas Jefferson. Jefferson was an Enlightenment rationalist who believed that "the alliance between church and state" produces only evil, and that a wall of separation must be maintained. His God was most certainly not the intervening Judeo-Christian God of the Bible. It was "Nature's God"—what the Jefferson scholar Allen Jayne calls the remote "watchmaker God of deism . . . who established the laws of nature at the time of creation and then left it alone."[9]

The last thing Jefferson—or John Adams, or Benjamin Franklin—intended was a government "built wholly on a Judeo-Christian foundation." Jefferson railed against such a concept from the moment he penned the Declaration; his next great project was a bill protecting religious freedom in Virginia. And Adams signed a treaty when he was president that explicitly declared that "the government of the United States is not in any sense founded on the Christian religion."[10]

The drafters of our eighteenth-century Declaration of Independence could not have had more different views from those held by today's Falwells, Robertsons, Dobsons, Keyeses, Liebermans, and Novaks. Indeed, as will become evident from a review of the relevant history, Jefferson intended his Declaration to free us not only from the political oppression of Great Britain but also from the religious oppression of evangelical clergymen who elevate "monkish ignorance and superstition" over the "unbound exercise of reason" and "the light of science." He certainly did not accept the insulting notion that there could be no virtue without religion, since he did not care whether anyone, even those closest to him, believed or disbelieved in God, as long as they relied on their own reason, and not the dogma of others, in reaching their decision. As Brooke Allen has summarized the history of that age:

> The eighteenth century was not an age of faith but an age of science and skepticism, and the American Founding Fathers were in its vanguard. As the philosopher Louis Dupré has uncompromisingly stated, "Our [Western] institutions and laws, our conception of the state, and our political sensitivity all stem from Enlightenment ideas. This, of course, is particularly true in the United States, where the Founding Fathers transformed those ideas into an unsurpassed system of balanced government." Even to their contemporaries this seemed obvious: the American Revolution, and the subsequent creation of the United States, embodied the Enlightenment values that had been formulated over the previous century. While some (though certainly not all) of the American colonies had originally been founded as religious communities—the Massachusetts Bay colony, chartered in 1629, was the major example of this sort of scheme—the ultimate confederation of the thirteen very different colonies as the United States was a purely secular project.[11]

In sum, the Declaration of Independence was designed to protect us from exactly that kind of Christianized America advocated by those who are now seeking to hijack the Declaration for their own sectarian purposes. The prominent historian Pauline Maier has put it this way:

As the heirs of a political tradition shaped by radical seventeenth-century English Protestants, most American revolutionaries were suspicious of Roman Catholicism and its iconographic traditions. Many went further and opposed the use of religion to reinforce the power of the state in any way: Indeed, separation of church and state was one of the most radical innovations of the American Revolution.[12]

Jefferson's Nonbiblical God of Nature

The Judeo-Christian God—Jehovah of the Old Testament and the Father of Jesus in the New Testament—was *not* the God Jefferson was referring to as Nature's God or the Creator.[13] Jefferson explicitly rejected the biblical God—"the Lord mighty in battle," the God who intervened in the lives of human beings, performed miracles, wrote the Bible, or had a son. Jefferson did not believe in divine revelation, the virgin birth, the Trinity, or the other fundamental theological underpinnings of Christianity. According to the historian Allen Jayne, the author of a recent, definitive study on Jefferson's theology, Jefferson rejected "orthodox Christian doctrine" and "before and during the time he drafted the Declaration of Independence, manifested a concealed 'hatred for ceremonial institutionalized Christianity.'"[14] Nor did he believe that Jesus was anything other than an ordinary human being or that Moses received the

Ten Commandments from God. Jefferson's "watchmaker" God did not answer human prayers.

Most important, although Jefferson's words are currently invoked by "people of faith"—as members of the Religious Right refer to themselves—Jefferson himself was the opposite of a person of faith. He rejected all reliance on conventional religious notions of "faith" based on revelation, miracles, or dogma. These concepts were anathema to him. Instead, he insisted that "human reason" was supreme, and if a person could not be convinced of a fact—including the existence of God—by reason alone, he should not accept that fact on the basis of faith, revelation, or dogma. In 1787 he wrote about the study of religion to his seventeen-year-old nephew Peter Carr, to whom he was proposing a complete course of study. Because this letter outlines Jefferson's views on religion perhaps more completely than any other single document, it warrants extensive quotation:

> Your reason is now mature enough to examine this object [religion]. In the first place, divest yourself of all bias in favor of novelty and singularity of opinion. On the other hand, shake off all the fears and servile prejudices, under which weak minds are servilely crouched. Fix reason firmly in her seat, and call to her tribunal every fact, every opinion. *Question with boldness even the existence of God; because, if there be one, he must more approve of the homage of reason, than that of blindfolded fear.* You will naturally examine first, the religion of your own country. Read the Bible, then, as you would read Livy or Tacitus. The facts which are within the ordinary course of nature, you will believe on the authority of the writer, as you do those of the same kind in Livy and Tacitus. The testimony of the writer weighs in their favor, in one scale,

and their not being against the laws of nature, does not weigh against them. But those facts in the Bible which contradict the laws of nature, must be examined with more care, and under a variety of faces. Here you must recur to the pretensions of the writer to inspiration from God. Examine upon what evidence his pretensions are founded, and whether that evidence is so strong, as that its falsehood would be more improbable than a change in the laws of nature, in the case he relates. For example, in the book of Joshua, we are told, the sun stood still several hours. Were we to read that fact in Livy or Tacitus, we should class it with the showers of blood, speaking of statues, beasts, etc. But it is said, that the writer of that book was inspired. Examine, therefore, candidly, evidence there is of his having been inspired. The pretension is entitled to your inquiry, because millions believe it. On the other hand, you are astronomer enough to know how contrary it is to the law of nature that a body revolving on its axis, as the earth does, should have stopped, should not, by that sudden stoppage, have prostrated animals, trees, buildings, and should after a certain time have resumed its revolution, and that without a second general prostration. Is this arrest of the earth's motion, or the evidence which affirms it, most within the law of probabilities? You would next read the New Testament. It is a history of a personage called Jesus. Keep in your eye the opposite pretensions: 1, of those who say he was begotten by God, born of a virgin, suspended and reversed the laws of nature at will, and ascended bodily into heaven; and 2, of those who say he was a man of illegitimate birth, of a benevolent heart, enthusiastic mind, who set out without pretensions to divinity, ended in believing them, and was punished capitally for sedition, by being gibbeted, according to the Roman law, which punished the first commission of that offence by whipping, and the second by exile, or death *in fureu.* . . .

Do not be frightened from this inquiry by any fear of its consequences. If it ends in a belief that there is no God, you will find incitements to virtue in the comfort and pleasantness you feel in its exercise, and the love of others which it will procure you. If you find reason to believe there is a God, a consciousness that you are acting under his eye, and that he approves you, will be a vast additional incitement, if there be a future state, the hope of a happy existence in that increases the appetite to deserve it; if that Jesus was also a God, you will be comforted by a belief of his aid and love. In fine, I repeat, you must lay aside all prejudice on both sides, and neither believe nor reject anything, because any other persons, or description of persons, have rejected or believed it. *Your own reason is the only oracle given you by Heaven, and you are answerable, not for the rightness, but the uprightness of the decision.* [Emphases added.][15]

It is impossible to conclude from this letter—in which Jefferson tells his own nephew that he would "find incitements to virtue" in "a belief that there is no God"—that Jefferson was among those self-righteous religious bigots who suggest that a person without religion cannot be virtuous. Indeed, in drafting his bill for establishing religious freedom in Virginia, Jefferson wrote that "our civil rights have no dependence on our religious opinions any more than our opinions in physics or geometry."[16] Just as no one could rationally argue that one's views on geometry bear any relationship to one's virtue, it fol-

lowed for Jefferson that one's views on God bear no relationship to one's virtue as well.

The letter also demonstrates that Jefferson rejected Pascal's
cynical wager—that it is a better bet to believe in a nonexist-
ent God than to risk damnation from an existing one—as well
as the anti-intellectual God who would reward a crass cost-
benefit analysis that led to belief in Him, while punishing an
honest inquiry that led to skepticism or disbelief. Just as no
God worthy of respect would punish a person for not believing in Euclidean geometry, so, too, no just God would punish
a thinking person for not believing in Him. I could never
comprehend the justice or rationality of any religious view
that limited salvation—or any kind of religious reward—to
those who believe in God or a particular savior. If there is a
God and he is just, he must reward those who honestly struggle with the mystery of his existence and arrive at the "wrong"
answer, as Jefferson believed. Life cannot be a betting parlor
with heaven as payoff for winning a wager.

Jefferson believed that a certain level of maturity was
required for the objective study of religion. Accordingly, he
opposed Bible study or reading by young students, arguing in
his *Notes on the State of Virginia* that "instead . . . of putting
the Bible and Testament into the hands of the children at an
age when their judgments are not sufficiently matured for
religious enquiries, their memories may be stored with the
most useful facts from Grecian, Roman, European and American history."[17] He feared that young students would be sub-
jected to religious indoctrination rather than the kind of
open inquiry he thought essential to the study of religion.

Jefferson's own personal belief in a nonintervening God of
nature was the product of his reasoning and his evaluation of
the evidence available during the late eighteenth and early
nineteenth centuries (just as his "suspicion" that blacks were

inherently mentally inferior to whites was based on his reason and his limited experience as a slaveowner). He was willing to be persuaded that he was wrong as to these, and other, beliefs.

Jefferson's Rejection of "Faith" and "Revelation" in Favor of "Human Reason" and "Experience"

To Thomas Jefferson, the important distinction was not between those who believed in God and those who did not. The important difference, as he explained to his nephew, was between those who arrived at their conclusion regarding God by human reason rather than by "faith," "dogma," "revelation," or other "unscientific" or "supernatural" means. Jefferson, along with most of his intellectual mentors and peers, rejected what Thomas Paine referred to in *The Age of Reason* as the "imaginary thing called faith."[18] Instead, they observed the available evidence and employed their own reason to conclude that God, in fact, existed. For them, belief in God did not require, or even permit, a "leap of faith." It required a scientific inquiry, governed by reason, into the factual support for God's existence. Indeed, for some deists, the existence of God was more a matter of logic than science. For them, God was a product of a syllogism: The universe exists; it must have been created; if it was created, there must have been an original creator; we call that original creator by the name of God. "We are"—they reason—"therefore He must be." Yet Jefferson maintained that if another person's inquiry led that person to the opposite conclusion, he should follow his reasoning and not believe in God. Unlike Augustine, Jefferson trusted "in man."

Throughout his life, Jefferson elevated human *reason* over dogmatic *belief*, even—perhaps especially—belief in God. In his intellectual world, there was a null hypothesis that posited the nonexistence of God if evidence and human reason led to that conclusion. The Jefferson biographer Willard Sterne Randall writes that he had an "uncompromising belief in reason as the sole and final arbiter of knowledge and worth."[19] His early education and extensive reading had "liberated him from faith," according to Jayne, who wrote, "To him it was not sufficient to state 'I believe' and merely recite religious opinions without any rational justification. Such affirmations were the method of faith, and Jefferson, as an advocate of reason, thought that religious opinion should be justified by arguments born of reason."[20] This is the mind-set of the scientist and the skeptic, not the man of faith in divine revelation.

To many of his contemporaries, Jefferson's mind-set was also that of the "infidel," the "apostate," and the "heretic."[21] During Jefferson's first campaign for the presidency, his opponents declared him to be an "atheist" and argued that a vote for Jefferson was, as his contemporary the Reverend William Linn put it, "no less than a rebellion against God." As proof of Jefferson's atheism, his own words of tolerance from the *Notes on the State of Virginia* were thrown back at him. There he had said, damningly in the minds of his detractors, "it does me no injury for my neighbor to say there are twenty gods, or no God."[22]

Jefferson as a "Man of the Bible"

As further proof of Jefferson's atheism, his disbelief in the alleged miracles recounted in the Bible was cited. Jefferson had "doubted the reality of the flood" and had "sinned in questioning the age of the earth."[23] He had even compared the supernatural myths of Christianity with those of the ancient Greeks and Romans, predicting that "the day will come when the mystical generation of Jesus by the Supreme Being as His Father, in the womb of a virgin, will be classed with the fable of the generation of Minerva in the brain of Jupiter."*[24] Jefferson not only disbelieved specific "mystical" accounts in the Bible, he also rejected "the mystical and metaphysical elements in Christianity, which he attributed to Plato's fuzzy thinking."[25]

Jefferson apparently derived many of his views about the Bible from other deists, and he shared many of Thomas Paine's criticisms of both the Old and the New Testaments. Paine—who was famous throughout the colonies for writing *Common Sense,* the pamphlet that helped inspire the revolution—also wrote *The Age of Reason,* a widely read book that savaged the Bible as a "pious fraud." Jefferson's analogy between biblical miracles and earlier mythological fables is similar to Paine's, who had based much of his criticism on the work of earlier deists. Paine repeatedly compared the miracles of the Bible to the supernatural accounts contained in Greek and Roman mythology. Indeed, he argued—quite persuasively—that the stories in the New Testament were, in fact, copied from earlier "heathen" accounts. Paine wrote of the virgin birth: "This story is upon the face of it, the same kind of story of Jupiter and Leda and Jupiter and Europa or any of the amorous adventures of Jupiter; and shows . . . that the Christian faith is built upon the heathen mythology."[26]

Paine went on to explain why Christians were prepared to believe the supernatural account of Jesus' birth:

---

*He probably would have approved also of Keith Preston's doggerel:
    The great god Ra, whose shrine once covered acres,
    is filler now for crossword puzzle makers.

It is, however, not difficult to account for the credit that was given to the story of Jesus Christ being the Son of god. He was born at a time when the heathen mythology had still some fashion and repute in the world, and that mythology had prepared the people for the belief of such a story. Almost all the extraordinary men that lived under the heathen mythology were reputed to be some of the sons of their gods. It was not a new thing, at that time, to believe a man to have been celestially begotten: the inter-course of gods with women was then a matter of familiar opinion. Their Jupiter according to their accounts, had cohabited with hundreds; the story therefore, had nothing in it neither new, wonderful, or obscene; it was conform-able to opinions that then prevailed among the people called Gentiles or Mythologists and it was these people only that believed it. The Jews who had kept strictly to the belief in one God and who had always rejected the hea-then mythology never credited the story. [Paine was not quite accurate. The Old Testament, in fact, contains sto-ries about gods mating with humans. See Genesis 5:4.][27]

Paine concluded, therefore, that "the theory of what is called the Christian church sprung out of the tail of heathen mythol-ogy."[28] He argued that "a direct incorporation took place in the first instance by making the reputed founder celestially begotten."[29] He also believed that the

trinity of gods that then followed was no other than a reduction of the former plurality. . . . The statue of Mary succeeded the statue of Diana of Ephesus. The deifica-tion of heroes changed into the canonization of saints. The Mythologists had gods for everything: the Christian Mythologists had saints for everything; the church became as crowded with the one as the Pantheon had been with the other, and Rome was the place of both.[30]

Paine's ultimate conclusion was a scathing attack on the Christian church:

> Of all the systems of religion that ever were invented, there is none more derogatory to the Almighty, more unedifying to man, more repugnant to reason, and more contradictory in itself, than this thing called Christianity. Too absurd for belief, too impossible to convince, and too inconsistent for practice, it renders the heart torpid, or produces only atheists and fanatics. As an engine of power, it serves the purpose of despotism; and as a means of wealth, the avarice of priests; but so far as respects the good of man in general, it leads to nothing here or hereafter.[31]

He continued: "The Christian theory is little else than idolatry of the ancient Mythologists; accommodated to the purpose of power and revenue; and it yet remains to reason and philosophy to abolish the amphibious fraud."[32] He concluded that "the Bible and the Testament are impositions on the world, that the fall of man, the account of Jesus Christ being the Son of God, and of his dying to appease the wrath of God, and of salvation by that strange means, are all fabulous inventions and dishonorable to the wisdom and power of Almighty."[33]

Paine and many of the other deists had similar criticisms of the Old Testament, a book that Paine regarded as "spurious." He was even critical of the Ten Commandments, which he argued "carry no internal evidence of divinity within them."[34] He acknowledged that they contain some good moral precepts, "such as any man qualified to be a lawgiver or a legislator, could produce himself, without having recourse to supernatural intervention."[35] But as to one provision contained in the Ten Commandments—"that God visits the sins of the father upon the children"—Paine argued that "it is contrary to every principle of moral justice."[36]

Jefferson also disbelieved in the divine origin of the Ten Commandments, asking in an 1824 letter to John Adams:

Where did we get the ten commandments? The book indeed give them to us verbatim, but where did it get them? For itself tells us they were written by the finger of God on tables of stone, which were destroyed by Moses; it specifies those on the second set of tables in different form and substance, but still without saying how the other were recovered. But the whole history of these books is so defective and doubtful, that it seems vain to attempt minute inquiry into it; and such tricks have been played with their text, and with the other texts of other books relating to them, that we have a right from that cause to entertain much doubt what parts of them are genuine.[37]

Jefferson had special contempt for the writers of the Gospels, whom he considered to be "ignorant, unlettered men." He regarded these writers as impostors, false witnesses, and corrupters of the true teachings of Jesus. He described "the stupidity of some, and roguery of other of His disciples."[38] He characterized the descriptions of Jesus' life as "a groundwork of vulgar ignorance, of things impossible, of superstitions, fanaticism, and fabrications."[39] He found it hard to believe that the Gospels, which contained "so much ignorance, so much absurdity, so much untruth, charlatanism and imposture," could have come from "the same being" who wrote the moral portions of these books. The words of Jesus he called "diamonds," and the words of his disciples he called "dung." According to Jaroslav Pelikan, a leading scholar in the history of Christianity, it was Jefferson's view that "the real villain in the Christian story was the apostle Paul, who had corrupted the religion of Jesus into a religion about Jesus, which thus had, in combination with the otherworldly outlook of the Fourth gospel produced the monstrosities of dogma, superstition, and priest craft, which were the essence of Christian orthodoxy."[40] Jefferson believed that Jesus was "the greatest of all the reformers of the depraved religion of his own country," and that Paul was the "first corrupter of the doctrines of Jesus."[41]

Jefferson's Views of Jesus and "Christ"

Although he considered himself a Christian—in the sense of approving of many of Jesus' *human* qualities—Jefferson, in fact, disagreed with the core of his religious and moral teachings. Here is how Jefferson himself put it: "It is not to be understood that I am with him in all his doctrines. I am a Materialist; he takes the side of Spiritualism. He preaches the efficacy of repentance towards the forgiveness of sin; I require a counterpoise of good works to redeem it, etc., etc."[42] Jefferson also regarded himself as "an Epicurean." He considered the "genuine . . . doctrines of Epicurus as containing everything rational in moral philosophy which Greece and Rome left us."[43] Epicurus preached that "pleasure is the beginning and end of the blessed life"[44]—a very un-Christian notion. Jefferson agreed, saying "that a hedonistic 'pursuit of happiness' was not inconsistent with an 'innate moral sense,'"[45] and he himself lived a life of both reflection and hedonism, one that eventually drove him to the brink of bankruptcy.

In addition to disagreeing with Jesus' central doctrines of spirituality and redemption, Jefferson made it clear that he explicitly rejected "the immaculate conception of Jesus, His deification, the creation of the world by Him, His miraculous powers, His resurrection and visible ascension, His corporal Presence in the Eucharist, the Trinity, original sin, atonement, regeneration, election, Orders of Hierarchy, etc."[46] He had particular disdain for the concept of the Trinity, characterizing it as "incomprehensible, unintelligible and insane."[47] He called it "the mere Abracadabra of the mountebanks calling themselves priests of Jesus."[48] He revered the writings of Joseph Priestley, who argued that the Trinity was a corruption based on a comparison between Jesus as the Son of God and "Mercury, Jupiter's Son."[49] Jefferson did not believe "in the existence of the traditional Christian heaven and hell,"[50] in the concept of "being saved,"[51] or in "grace."[52] He was "influenced by the Roman stoics to view suicide with sympathy,"[53] despite the Christian prohibition against taking one's own life. Most important, "It was a prime article of Jefferson's deistic religion that Jesus was not a deity."[54] In other words, Jefferson rejected all the central tenets of orthodox Christianity.

Indeed, it took some courage for Jefferson to express these heretical views, since under Virginia law, heresy was a serious crime. Any person raised as a Christian who denied the Trinity or the divine authority of Scripture could be disqualified from holding office and even have his children taken away and placed into more orthodox hands.

Beyond this, Jefferson's skepticism regarding Christianity was not limited to its supernatural aspects. Although he admired the teachings of Jesus, he did not believe that Jesus' philosophy, which was scattered through the Gospels, was anything more than an "unconnected system of ethics,"[55] which were "defective as a whole."[56] He contrasted the teachings of Jesus with the "writings of ancient heathen moralists,"[57] which he believed would be "more full, more entire, more coherent, and more clearly deduced from unquestionable principles of knowledge."

Was Jefferson Even a Christian?

Jefferson rarely attended church, and he viewed "the priest" —broadly defined to encompass all clerics—as "always in alliance with the despot, abetting his abuses in return for protection to his own."[58] He despised the sectarianism of the Christian churches:

> You may ask my opinion on the items of doctrine in your catechism. I have never permitted myself to mediate a specified creed. These formulas have been the bane and ruin of the Christian church, its own fatal invention, which, through so many ages, made of Christendom a slaughter-house, and at this day divides it into castes of inextinguishable hatred to one another.[59]

Yet despite his rejection of Christian dogma, Jefferson declared himself to be a Christian "in the only sense he [Jesus] wished anyone to be; sincerely attached to his doctrines in preference to all others; ascribing to himself every *human* excellence; and believing he never claimed any other" (emphasis added)[60]. In other words, he accepted *Jesus* (at least in part) while rejecting *Christ* (in every respect). It is difficult, therefore, to accept his claim to being a Christian, since the very word connotes acceptance of Jesus as the "Christos," the divinely anointed Messiah. In some of his private correspondence, he distinguished between deists like himself, on the one hand, and Christians, on the other.[61] It is likely that he publicly embraced the word "Christianity" for expedient political reasons, while rejecting its theological essence, for personal philosophical reasons. His critics called him an "opposer of Christianity,"[62] a man who had "a total disregard to public worship and an absolute indifference to religion whatsoever."[63] When he ran against John Adams for president, one newspaper put the choice as follows: GOD—AND A RELIGIOUS PRESIDENT OR . . . JEFFERSON—AND NO GOD.[64] Jefferson himself said, "I am of a sect by myself, as far as I know."[65]

Would Jefferson Today Be Considered a "Secular Humanist" or a "Unitarian"?

Several of Jefferson's biographers have speculated about where Jefferson's views on religion would place him in today's world of religious categories. Jefferson variously considered himself a Christian, a deist, and a Unitarian. In 1822 he wrote the following:

> I rejoice that in this blessed country of free enquiry and belief, which has surrendered its creed and conscience to neither kings nor priests, the genuine doctrine of one only God is reviving, and I trust there is not a young man now living in the United States who will not die an Unitarian.[66]

The Jefferson scholar Allen Jayne wrote of Jefferson's possible Unitarianism that it

> was not only in accord with the use of individual critical reason in religion as espoused and put into practice by the Enlightenment and Jefferson; it was a product of the Enlightenment and critical reason. It would seem, therefore, that Jefferson regarded it as the religious counterpart of the University of Virginia, which Charles Sanford described as "an institution that would foster the

development of the ideals of the enlightenment by which he had lived all his life." Indeed, Unitarianism was perceived by Jefferson as a religion that corresponded generally with the theology of the Declaration of Independence and one that, like that theology, was conducive to the efficacy of the political theory of the document. As a religion based on individual reasons and judgment, it served and preserved the similarly based politics of the Declaration.[67]

Whether Unitarianism—which rejects much of Christian theological dogma—can be considered a Christian religion remains a hotly debated issue.

The biographer Joseph Ellis has said that "in modern day parlance, he was a secular humanist"[68]—a term of opprobrium to those of the contemporary Religious Right, who cite the words of Jefferson's Declaration in support of their fundamentalist agenda. He has been described as an Enlightenment rationalist, a religious skeptic, and a scientific believer in God by design. He also has been called a secularist and even the father of "the secularization of scientific research in America."[69] His political enemies accused him of being an infidel, especially since he continued to praise Thomas Paine even after Paine wrote his vitriolic attack on the Bible and Christianity in *The Age of Reason*. "Federalist newspaper editors had a field day describing 'the two Toms' walking arm in arm, allegedly comparing notes on the ideal way to promote atheism or their past successes in despoiling Christian virgins."[70] Dozens of pamphlets and articles characterized Jefferson as a "French infidel and atheist."[71] Alexander Hamilton, who himself had little use for religion, called Jefferson an "atheist and fanatic." Writings by and about Jefferson were banned from the Philadelphia public library until 1830 on the ground of his purported atheism. Even many years later, President Theodore Roosevelt attacked Paine as "a filthy little atheist."[72] But neither Jefferson nor Paine were atheists. They both accepted the God of Nature while rejecting the God of Judaism, Christianity, and Islam. Indeed, they viewed deism as a true religion capable of saving the world from the kind of atheistic reaction to Christianity that was being seen in France. Paine's justification for penning *The Age of Reason* was that he "was genuinely alarmed by the growth of atheism and was convinced that the growing disbelief in God and a future life was due primarily to the disgust men felt for the reactionary and rigid conduct of the clergy."[73]

Although Jefferson considered himself religious, he would not be so considered by some of today's religious thinkers. The Yale law professor Stephen Carter, for example, defines religion as "the belief in supernatural intervention in human affairs."[74] Such belief, according to Carter, "is a useful divider" because "this is where the culture seems to draw the line." There can be no question about on which side of that dividing line Jefferson's views fall.

Did Jefferson Believe in an Afterlife?

The reality is that Thomas Jefferson's views of religion were a hodgepodge of Enlightenment rationality, deism by design, political opportunism, and contradictions. They also changed over time, especially after he was attacked for being an atheist. One example of his contradictory theology lies in his belief in life after death, despite there being as little evidence for that conclusion as for the virgin birth, the resurrection, or the divine origin of the Ten Commandments. Yet life after death was a firm tenet of much of the deism of the day, even that of Thomas Paine, who wrote, "I hope for happiness beyond this life."[75] Paine's "scientific" arguments for an afterlife are embarrassingly unscientific:

> I content myself with believing, even to positive conviction, that the Power that gave me existence is able to continue it, in any form and manner He pleases, either with or without this body . . .[76]
>
> . . . A very numerous part of the animal creation preaches to us, far better than Paul, the belief of a life hereafter. Their little life resembles an earth and a heaven—a present and a future state, and comprises, if it may be so expressed, immortality in miniature.
>
> The most beautiful parts of the creation to our eye are the winged insects, and they are not so originally. They acquire that form and that inimitable brilliancy by progressive changes. The slow and creeping caterpillar-worm of to-day passes in a few days to a torpid figure and a state resembling death; and in the next change comes forth in all the miniature magnificence of life, a splendid butterfly.
>
> No resemblance of the former creature remains; everything is changed; all his powers are new, and life is to him another thing. We cannot conceive that the consciousness of existence is not the same in this state of the animal as before; why then must I believe that the resurrection of the same body is necessary to continue to me the consciousness of existence hereafter?[77]

Confusing metaphor with science, Paine hoped for a metamorphosis from his earthly body to some new form of existence in the hereafter.

What Paine merely hoped for, Jefferson seemed to accept,

especially as he grew older. He repeatedly wrote to friends that "we [shall] meet again in another place."[78] Some Jefferson scholars argue that his statements about an afterlife suggest approval of the concept as a practical spur to good deeds—"the great sanction"[79]—rather than as an actual belief: "As a student of law and history and a practicing attorney and statesman, he saw the importance of a belief in eternal judgment for encouraging a moral life of service to society."[80] Thus Jefferson's afterlife did not reward or punish based on "faith which is not within our power," but instead on "our good works which are within our power."[81]

If Jefferson's acceptance of an afterlife as a reward for good works was more a tactical way of encouraging good behavior than a deeply felt belief, he was certainly not alone—then or today. Many agnostics and atheists accept religion because they believe it does some good, even if it is based on a pious fraud. The case for religion as placebo is persuasive to many decent people. If others believe in God, an afterlife, or the efficacy of prayer, this set of beliefs may be beneficial to them, even if it turns out to be untrue. So why try to disabuse them of their false, though beneficial, beliefs? This approach to religion, or an afterlife, is akin to Pascal's wager: It is better to believe than to disbelieve in God, because if He does not exist and you believe He does, you have risked nothing, but if you do not believe in Him and He does exist, you will be punished in the afterlife (provided, of course, that God punishes you for your ultimate beliefs, even if they are the product of a cost-benefit calculation, rather than for your honest efforts to find the truth). Religion as placebo is less cynical than Pascal's wager but equally tactical.

There is also the related question of whether religion (or belief in God) is good or bad for society, regardless of whether it is "true" or "false." Even if every aspect of a given religion is totally bogus, the religion can produce much good, as the "false" religions of Greek, Roman, and Egyptian mythology did. The literature, art, philosophy, and architecture inspired by these "false" religions are every bit as great as those inspired by "true" religions. The religiously inspired music of Bach is as beautiful whether God exists or not, or whether Jesus is or is not the Savior. I get emotional every time I listen to the finale of Verdi's *Requiem*, even though I (and Verdi) believe not a word of its text.

There are various conclusions a rational person can reach about religion, among which are the following:

- It is true and produces good.
- It is true and produces bad or mixed results.
- It is false and produces good.
- It is false and produces bad or mixed results.
- It cannot be known whether it is true, but it can be known that it produces good, bad, or mixed results.

Jefferson seemed to conclude that belief in God was true and produced good results, that belief in the supernatural and institutional aspects of organized religion is false and produces bad results, and that belief in reward and punishment after death is unprovable but produces good results—if judgment is based on deeds rather than beliefs.

Jefferson often wrote of the "pillow of ignorance" on which he was willing to rest his uncertain brain when it came to issues about which people could not be sure, including life after death.[82] Jefferson saw Jesus' promise of life after death as a major improvement over what he mistakenly believed was the Jewish view: "He [Jesus], taught, emphatically, the doctrines of a future state, which was either doubted or disbelieved by the Jews; and wheedled it with efficacy, as an important incentive, supplementary to the other motives to moral conduct."[83] Jefferson was correct about biblical Judaism, but he was apparently ignorant of rabbinic Judaism, which for several hundred years before the birth of Jesus had insisted on life after death. Indeed, Jefferson's critique of Judaism as lacking concern for humanity as a whole was ignorant of the writings of Jesus' predecessors such as Rabbi Hillel, who foreshadowed many of Jesus' statements about the love of all humanity. Hillel, some years before Jesus, had famously responded to the challenge to teach the whole Pentateuch standing on one leg by saying: "That which is despicable to you, do not do to your fellow, this is the whole Torah, and the rest is commentary."[84] Jefferson was thus apparently unaware that Jesus was expressing a traditional Jewish view when he wrote, "To love God with all thy heart and thy neighbor as thyself is the sum of religion."[85] Indeed, if Jesus was neither the son of God nor a supernatural figure of any kind—as Jefferson firmly believed he was not—then an apt characterization of this great human being is that he was the first Reform rabbi, a Jew who rejected much of the ritualistic aspects of traditional Judaism in favor of its more spiritual and ethical teachings, which he elaborated, adapted, and extended. Jefferson might well have been comfortable with such a characterization of the very human Jesus in whose teachings he believed.

Jefferson's "Argument by Design" for the Existence of Nature's God

Jefferson's argument for God "by the design of nature" is popular today among fundamentalists who seek to use science to prove the existence of God. This is how Jefferson explained his scientific approach to John Adams:

> I hold, (without appeal to revelation) that when we take a view of the universe, in its parts, general or particular, it is impossible for the human mind not to perceive and feel a conviction of design, consummate skill, and indefinite power in every atom of its composition. The movements of the heavenly bodies, so exactly held in their course by the balance of centrifugal and centripetal forces; the structure of our earth itself, with its distribution of lands, waters and atmosphere; animal and vegetable bodies, examined in all their minutest particles; insects, mere atoms of life, yet as perfectly organized as man or mammoth; . . . it is impossible, I say, for the human mind not to believe, that there is in all this, design, cause and effect, up to an ultimate cause, a Fabricator of all things from matter and motion.[86]

David Hume had earlier responded to the "argument by design" in the following way:

> Look around this universe. What an immense profusion of beings, animated and organized, sensible and active! You admire this prodigious variety and fecundity. But inspect a little more narrowly these living existences. . . . How hostile and destructive to each other! . . . The whole presents nothing but the idea of a blind nature, impregnated by a great vivifying principle, and pouring forth from her lap, without discernment or parental care, her maimed and abortive children.[87]

A century later, Darwin was to provide a systematic, scientific basis for Hume's observation.

In my book *Shouting Fire* I elaborate on Hume's argument as follows:

The reality is that nature is morally neutral. It is full of beauty and wonder, but it thrives on violence and predation. Nature is a mother animal nursing her helpless cub and then killing another helpless animal to survive. Nature is life-giving sunshine followed by death-dealing floods. Human nature is Albert Schweitzer and Adolf Hitler, Jesus and Torquemada, Kant and Nietzsche, Confucius and Pol Pot, Mandela and bin Laden, the early Martin Luther, who reached out to the despised, and the later Martin Luther, who advocated rounding up the Jews and making them "miserable captives" in forced-labor camps.

In constructing a moral code—or a system of rights— one should not ignore the varieties of human nature, or their alleged commonalities. But neither can the diverse components of nature be translated directly into morality, legality, or rights. The complex relationship between the *is* of nature and the *ought* of morality must be mediated by human experience.[88]

For honest proponents of the "argument by design"— those who seek the objective truth wherever it may take them, rather than those who seek to "prove" an already accepted premise—the conclusion may change over time. The "argument by design" is an argument of exclusion: There *must* be a god, because there is no *other* plausible explanation for the benign design of the world. As Prat de Lamartine was to put it several generations after Jefferson: "God—but a word invoked to explain the world." Indeed, it is uncertain whether Jefferson and his fellow deists would have arrived at their deistic conclusion if they were aware of current scientific explanations of how the world came about. In the wake of the discoveries of Darwin, Einstein, and others, many deists became agnostics or atheists. That is the "danger" of the "argument by design" and why so many people of faith reject it as dangerous: it makes belief in God dependent on the progress of science in filling in gaps, rendering it decreasingly likely that God is needed as science explains more and more. The God of design is the diminishing God of the diminishing gaps. Although there will always be gaps in our collective knowledge of the universe—we are all "Newton's dog" when it comes to the origin of matter—we now understand that the existence of these gaps is itself explainable by science. It is not surprising that deism and belief in the God of Nature reached its peak after Galileo and Newton and began to decline after Darwin and Einstein.

For Jefferson, belief in the existence of Nature's God did not require a leap of faith; the real "leap"—to Jefferson, an irrational and illogical one—would be from God's existence to his authorship of the Bible, his revelation to selected humans, his performing of miracles, and his need for churches, prayers, and priests. There is nothing in the design of the world that could possibly lead a rational person to believe that God wrote a deeply flawed book filled with injustice, false-hoods, and unnatural occurrences. Indeed, if design *proved* God's existence, that same design—and the laws of nature governing it—would tend to disprove claims of supernatural, miraculous, and unobservable phenomena. Jefferson charac-terized the intervening Judeo-Christian God of miracles as "a bungling artist" who could not get it right in the first place. A true God would create rules of nature that did not require the help of supernatural miracles. Nor would a perfect God demand that people believe in him or build churches or establish religious hierarchies to worship him. He would judge each person, as Jefferson told his nephew, "not for the rightness" of his beliefs, but for the "uprightness" and honesty of the rational process by which it was reached.

Ultimately all scientific, empirical, or logical arguments for God's existence must fail under the accepted rules of science, empiricism, and logic. The only plausible argument for God is an unscientific, antiempirical, and illogical reliance on blind (deaf and dumb) *faith*—precisely the sort of faith Jefferson rejected. Pope Gregory I was wiser than Jefferson when he said, "If the work of God could be comprehended by reason, it would be no longer wonderful, and faith would have no merit if reason provided proof."

The critics of deism were right as a matter of empirical truth when they predicted that deism would inevitably lead to agnosticism (though that word had not yet been coined) and atheism. Paine and Jefferson were wrong in believing that deism would save religion from atheism. Any belief in God that is based on science, empiricism, and logic will eventually lead to doubt about or disbelief in God. Indeed, any religious claim that purports to be provable or disprovable by the canons of science—whether it is deism, creationism, literal belief in miracles, or the end of the world at a predicted time—will end up in the wastebin of history, along with the geocentric theory, the authenticity of the Shroud of Turin, and the Bible Codes. Science will never prove religion to be true, and if religion submits its empirical claims to scientific proof, it will prove them false.

As our knowledge gap narrows, belief in God's existence can survive only if it lays claims to a magisterium outside of science,[89] and many contemporary religious leaders understand this far better than Jefferson did. Jefferson was naive in believing that science and rationality could discover God or prove his existence, because the object of science is to explain every phenomenon without recourse to the supernatural, the unempirical, or the illogical. The deus ex machina is outside of science. The most that science can ever say is, "We can explain this" or "we cannot yet explain that." It cannot take the next step—as Jefferson tried to do—and say, "Since we cannot explain it, it must be the work of a God" or some other supernatural phenomenon outside the magisterium of science. Individual scientists may, of course, accept faith and believe in God without trying to prove God's existence scientifically. But in his effort to replace faith and revelation with rationality and science, Jefferson laid the foundation for skepticism, agnosticism, and secularism—even if that was not his intention.

In a class I teach at Harvard that deals with religion, science, philosophy, and law, I try to test the proposition—rejected by Jefferson but espoused by my late colleague Stephen Jay Gould and my coteacher Harvey Cox—that religion and science occupy separate magisteria: that the former deals with normative issues of morality, while the latter deals with empirical issues of fact. I try to challenge the sharpness of this separation by arguing that for many religious people, their "faith" is actually based on the empirical conclusion that certain "events"—that are central to their religion—actually took place. I pose two hypothetical scenarios to the students who profess faith in the Christian, Jewish, or Muslim religion. The first posits a camera on a galaxy several thousand light-years away that can send images back to Earth much faster than the speed of light—in fact, instantaneously. The camera is focused on Sinai, Calvary, and the Dome of the Rock and proves to the complete empirical satisfaction of the students that no Ten Commandments were given to Moses on Sinai, that Jesus was not resurrected, and that Muhammad did not ascend to heaven with his horse.

The second hypothetical scenario asks students to imagine

that they are on a dig in the Qumran Caves outside of Jerusalem, where the original Dead Sea Scrolls were discovered. In a distant part of a previously unexplored cave, one of the students discovers a new scroll sealed in a jug. He has with him a machine capable of determining the age and authenticity of the scroll. It proves to be authentic. He opens it up and reads it in the original language. It is the proceedings of a conclave of ancient priests who are trying to get their people to be more moral and law-abiding. They discuss various options, and the high priest comes up with the idea of staging an event on top of a mountain at which a man dressed up to look like God gives another man, posing as a prophet, two tablets containing Ten Rules of Conduct. "The people will have to follow those rules if they believe that God Himself wrote them," the high priest declares. All agree, and they proceed to debate what the Ten Rules should be. (Variations on this hypothetical can include a staged resurrection or a staged ascent to heaven on a horse.)

I ask whether such proof—believed to be empirically true—would shake their faith in their religion. In other words, how much, if any, of the religious faith of the students is based on the actual occurrence of the central events in their faith's religious narrative? Many students hate the question. They fight with the hypothetical: How can I be sure the camera is accurate or the scroll is authentic? You're sure! Maybe God doesn't want us to look back at history. Maybe He wants us to believe on the basis of faith. Okay, then, this is a good test: Do you believe on faith even if you're convinced the story is factually false, even fraudulent?

Finally, the students express their opinions. A considerable number of them—usually more than half—say their faith would be shaken or destroyed if the empirical basis for it was conclusively disproved. Even more say it would be destroyed by proof of knowing fraud—even well-intentioned "pious fraud."

It seems clear from Jefferson's reliance on human observation, the laws of nature, and human reason that he would not regard these testing cases as difficult: they would confirm his conclusions about the mistaken or fraudulent nature of "revelations" and "miracles." Nor would these hypotheticals shake his belief in a nonintervening God of Nature. What might shake his belief would be the findings of scientists who could fill gaps in explaining the design of the world without recourse to a God. New scientific findings might have caused him, as they caused many others, to reconsider his reliance on the argument by design for God's existence. Though the test would be different for Jefferson from that of some of my students, the process and outcome would be similar: If belief in God or religion is based on science and rationality, then the same science and rationality will eventually shake those beliefs in any person who truly has an open mind. Science and rationality, by their nature, are double-edged swords when it comes to God and religion, and playing with such swords can be dangerous to beliefs.

The difference between Jefferson and contemporary fundamentalists is that Jefferson, despite his own conclusion that it was "impossible" not to believe in "a Fabricator of all things from matter and motion," seemed open to the possibility that science might lead him, or others, away from belief in God— certainly a benevolent God. Contemporary fundamentalists, on the other hand, begin with a constant: God's existence (plus a whole lot of other beliefs, such as the divine authorship of the Bible). They use—misuse—science as a *prop* to try to convince others of what they already "know" to be true. If science were to fail to prove the existence of God, then they would assert that science was inadequate to the task. God's existence is the premise and the constant. Everything else is variable. I know some Jews who grasp at every new archaeological finding that lends any support, no matter how flimsy, to certain biblical accounts, and scoff at the absence of findings to support other biblical accounts, claiming that the absence of evidence is not evidence of absence. So, too, when science suggests that there may be benefits from the dietary laws of kashrut or the ritual laws of circumcision, these findings are trumpeted. But if science suggests no benefit, they quietly deny that these rules were designed to produce physical benefits. Heads I win, tails you lose!

Indeed, the foolishness of trying to prove the existence of God through the use of science, especially for a Christian, is evidenced by a clear contradiction between that project and the traditional Christian view of reward and punishment in the afterlife. The Christian view traditionally offers hope of salvation only to those who end up believing in God (not to mention an assortment of other supernatural phenomena). But if belief in God is to be based on empirical observation, it would be entirely irrational to attach any moral opprobrium to reaching an "erroneous" scientific conclusion based on an honest search for truth. Traditional Christians cannot have it both ways: they must either give up on claiming that belief in God is based on science; or they must give up on claiming that God will punish you for not believing in Him. Jefferson gave up on the latter.

The other important difference between Jefferson and today's fundamentalists of all religious persuasions is that Jefferson distinguished between the existence of God, which he accepted, and the miracles of the Bible, which he rejected. For Jefferson, the latter did not follow from the former, as it does—so illogically—for many fundamentalists. Jefferson, as I pointed out, believed that "miracles"—purported deviations from Laws of Nature—were inconsistent with the God of

Nature who created the rules of Nature and would not deviate from them, as he believed that the imperfect and often unjust laws of the Bible would be inconsistent with a benevolent and just God.

There is, of course, no rational relationship between the existence of a God and his purported authorship or inspiration of any particular book, whether it be the Old or New Testament, the Koran, the Book of Mormon, or any other "sacred" script. Even if God does exist—whether He is a passive watchmaker, an active intervener, or something else—it simply does not follow that He wrote or inspired any of these books, spoke to any of the alleged prophets, or performed any of the miracles reported in these books. To be sure, if there is no God, it would follow that these books, conversations, and miracles are human contrivances, but it would not follow from the existence of God that they were not.

The essence of deism was a strong belief, based on design, in the existence of a God of Nature, and an even stronger belief that this God bears absolutely no relationship to, or responsibility for, the very flawed books and unjust actions attributed to him, or the historically corrupt churches that claim to be doing his bidding. The logical fallacy engaged in by those who would leap from the mention of God in the Declaration to the conclusion that this document was intended to accept the Judeo-Christian biblical narrative lies in their failure to understand the God-Bible non sequitur. The historical error lies in their refusal to acknowledge that the deists who drafted the Declaration believed in the nonintervening God of Nature who created the world but did not write the Bible, father Jesus, or have anything to do with Christianity, Judaism, or any other organized religion or church. Since deism—at least in name—is no longer a popular religious position, it is easier to make the mistake of associating belief in God with belief in the Judeo-Christian, or some other, organized religious dogma.

Jefferson's Views Regarding Religion in the Public Square

Jefferson was categorically opposed to public profession of religious beliefs by public figures or government officials. Indeed, according to his biographer Dumas Malone, Jefferson "made no effort to clarify his own position or make his personal religious opinions known [because] he regarded this as a wholly private matter which was nobody's business but his." [90] As he wrote to the son of a close friend, "Religion [is] a subject on which I have ever been most scrupulously reserved. I have considered it as a matter between every man and his maker in which no other, and far less the public has a right to intermeddle." [91]

In selecting portions of Jesus' teachings that he admired and believed in, Jefferson included the following:

> and when thou prayest, thou shalt not be as the hypocrites are: for they love to pray standing in the synagogues and in the corners of the streets, that they may be seen of men . . . but thou, when thou prayest, enter into thy closet, and when thou hast shut thy door, pray to thy Father which is in secret . . . but when ye pray use not then repetitions as the heathen do: for they think they shall be heard for their much speaking. [92]

It is not surprising, therefore, that Jefferson said, "I am moreover adverse to the communication of my religious tenets to the public." He urged public figures to refuse to answer "questions of faith, which the laws have left between

God and [themselves]."[93] And as president he refused "to proclaim a national Thanksgiving Day in order not to influence religious practices of the country's people."[94] There are some, like Akhil Reed Amar and Stephen Carter, who argue that Jefferson was opposed only to the establishment of religion by the federal government, leaving it to each state to decide whether to have an established church, but this is incorrect. He fought to disestablish the Anglican Church in Virginia on principles that were universally applicable, and "was thrilled in 1818 when the Presbyterian Church was removed as Connecticut's established church."[95] Indeed, his entire philosophy opposed the intermingling of politics with religion at any level of government. He expressed "opposition to any form of civil religious observances."[96] It is clear from these, and other similar statements throughout Jefferson's correspondence, that he would be deeply offended by modern politicians who wear their religion on their sleeves and who compete to outdo other politicians in their public proclamations of devotion to their religious faith. These are indeed the "hypocrites" who want their devotion to be "seen of men"—especially voters.

Those who cite the Declaration of Independence as proof that Jefferson believed in public avowals of religion should be reminded that to Jefferson, as Willard Sterne Randall put it, "religion was a private matter, like marriage, and in 1776 he said little about his private views on the subject. He did not attend church frequently, eschewed religious dogma, and believed in a supreme being who had set the world on its foundation and stepped aside."[97] He viewed the clergy of all organized religion as corrupt, fraudulent, and dishonest—accusing them of promoting false religions. He rejected any reliance on the Bible by judges and rejected the notion—then quite prevalent—that Christianity or the Bible were part of the common law. As previously noted, he characterized such reliance as judicial "usurpation" and railed against the incorporation into English law of "laws made for the Jews alone, and the precepts of the [Christian] gospel."[98] He opposed "reading of the Bible by schoolchildren,"[99] and there can be little doubt that he would have opposed the posting of the Ten Commandments in public schools, especially those that commanded the worship of a particular God in a particular way and threatened punishment of children for the sins of their fathers. Indeed even today, almost nobody proposes that the full "Ten Commandments" actually be posted in schools or courthouses. What they want posted are the "Ten Bumper Stickers" or "Cliff's Notes"—abbreviated renditions of the actual commandments, since the full text contains reference to slavery, intergenerational punishment, and conflicting reasons for observing a day of rest on Saturday, not Sunday. Even this, though, would have been anathema to Jefferson's secularist views on both education and civil life.

Jefferson regarded his second-greatest contribution to the world—the first being his authorship of the Declaration of Independence—to be his work on the Virginia Statute on Religious Freedom, which, in his words, "produced the first legislature who had the courage to declare that the reason of man may be trusted with the formation of his own opinion," thereby freeing the human from the "vassalage" in which it has been held for "so many ages" by "kings, priests and nobles."[100] He railed against laws that imposed religious tests of any kind, characterizing them as part of our long history of "religious slavery." He included atheists as within the protection of religious liberty. His third-greatest contribution was the establishment of a secular university that would, according to the authors of *The Godless Constitution*, Isaac Kramnick and R. Laurence Moore, "preserve the wall of separation intact. It would be America's first truly secular university, having no religious instruction, other than as a branch of ethics, and no professor of divinity."[101] It may be difficult for the contemporary mind, so accustomed to today's secular university, to grasp the revolutionary nature of Jefferson's secular university at the time it was proposed. All higher education in eighteenth-century America was completely under the domination of clerics, and Jefferson's radical proposal was widely condemned by the clergy. Even as late as 1900, the president of Trinity College, subsequently renamed Duke University, urged Southerners not to send their children to colleges that were not church-sponsored. He characterized Jefferson's university as a marriage of "civil authority and infidelity" and "a deistic daring of enormous proportions." He called Jefferson "an infidel, agnostic and a materialist."[102]

More recently, the Reverend Jerry Falwell, in urging a "return" to the good old days, ignored Jefferson's secular school but was otherwise generally accurate in his description (though wrongheaded in his prescription):

> I hope to see the day when *as in the early days of our country,* we won't have any public schools. The churches will have taken them over again and Christians will be running them. . . . We must never allow our children to forget that this is a Christian nation. We must take back what is rightfully ours.[103]

That is, of course, precisely what Jefferson was fighting against.

No one would be more surprised than Thomas Jefferson—except perhaps his contemporaneous detractors—at how he is being portrayed by today's right-wing orthodox Christians. They have the chutzpah to claim him as the champion of *their* God, *their* Bible, *their* Christianity, and *their* desire to break down the wall of separation between church and state. Jefferson would be stunned to see the Declaration itself being cited in support of public declarations of belief in the Judeo-Christian God. In his own time, Jefferson was seen, quite correctly, as a champion of the Enlightenment, as a critic of organized religion and a disbeliever in the divine authorship of the Bible and the theological doctrines of Christianity. Indeed, Charles B. Sanford, the author of *The Religious Life of Thomas Jefferson,* underlined that point in 1984—before recent efforts by the Religious Right to lay claim to the Declaration of Independence as a Judeo-Christian document:

> Over the years since Jefferson's death those who have favored official religious observances by governmental bodies and the public schools, as well as governmental aid to religious organizations, have often perceived Thomas Jefferson as the one most responsible for America's deplorable lack of religion.[104]

They may be correct in crediting Jefferson with opposing governmental involvement in religion, but they are wrong in blaming him for America's purported "lack of religion." It is the wall of separation between church and state, so strongly supported by Jefferson, that is largely responsible for religion thriving in this country, as compared to those European countries in which church and state have been united, resulting in opposition to the church by those who disapprove of the government. Jon Meacham reminds us of the views of the founders with regard to governmental support for religion: "'It is error alone which needs the support of government,' Jefferson said. 'Truth can stand by itself.' Franklin agreed: 'When a religion is good, I conceive that it will support itself; and, when it cannot support itself, and God does not take to support [it], so that its professors are obligated to call for help of the civil power, it is a sign, I apprehend, of its being a bad one.'"[105]

What Would Jefferson Think of Today's Religious Right?

It is always dangerous to speculate what any past historical figure would think about current issues, but in this case it seems beyond dispute that Jefferson would seek to uphold a high wall of separation between religion and government, church and state, "garden" and "wilderness." This metaphor of a "wall of separation between Church and State" derives from a letter Jefferson, as president, wrote to the Danbury Baptist Association in 1802, explaining why, as president, he would not proclaim a national fast day. In that letter he emphasized his firm belief that religion "is a matter which lies solely between man and his God" and that the powers of government do not extend to "opinions."[106] These were not transient notions—they were central to Jefferson's religious *and* political philosophy throughout his life. As a young lawyer, his most important case involved separation of church and state. He appended to his brief in that case "a disquitation" on why the doctrines of Christianity in particular and the Bible in general are not part of the common law. He wrote:

> In truth, the alliance between church and state in England, has ever made their judges accomplice in the frauds of clergy; and even bolder than they are; for instead of being contented with the surreptitious introduction of these four chapters of Exodus, they have taken the whole leap, and declared at once that the whole Bible and Testament, in a lump, make a part of

the common law of the land; the first judicial declaration which was by this Sir Matthew Hale. And thus they incorporate into the English code, laws made for the Jews alone, and the precepts of the gospel, intended by their benevolent author as obligatory only in *foro conscientiae*; and they arm the whole with the coercions of municipal law. They do this, too, in a case where the question was, not at all, whether Christianity was a part of the law of England, but simply how far the *ecclesiastical law* was to be respected by the common law courts of England, in the special case of a right of presentment. Thus identifying Christianity with the ecclesiastical law of England.[107]

The battlefield on which the war between Enlightenment rationalism and clerical fundamentalism was fought at the time of the Declaration of Independence was not over the existence of God, or even the mention of God in public declarations. Virtually every philosophical thinker in Jefferson's time believed in some kind of God, and virtually every public document invoked God in some form. Many even invoked Jesus. As Paine put it: "It is certain that, in one point, all the nations of the earth and all religions agree—all believe in a God."[108] The contentious divisions were over the *nature* of God, the *methodology* employed in deciding whether God existed, the *divinity of the Bible*, and the *role of churches*, ministers, and priests. In regard to *all* of these issues, Jefferson came down squarely against traditional religion and faith, and on the side of secular rationality. While his God was the God of Nature—a celestial watchmaker who performed no miracles, did not intrude into the lives of humans, and required no church or human intermediaries—the God of traditional religion was the God of miracles, the vengeful

Jehovah, the Lord "mighty in battle," the father of Jesus, the apex of the Christian Trinity. Jefferson's methodology rejected traditional notions of faith, revelation, and dogma in favor of science and human reason. As his letter to his nephew revealed, he did not care whether a person's reason led him to believe or disbelieve in God, as long as he backed his conclusion on reason and observation. He rejected proselytizing. He was even reticent about letting his ideas on religion influence his own family.[109]

As his own writings demonstrate, Jefferson was convinced beyond any doubt that both the Old and New Testaments—especially the parts that describe miracles, revelations, and other supernatural phenomena—were pious frauds (he was less certain that they were pious than that they were frauds). Finally, he had no use for churches, ministers, priests, and the doctrines of organized religion. He was "anticlerical" and "rejected the moral authority of the clergy,"[110] observing that "history . . . furnishes no example of a priest-ridden people maintaining a free civil government"[111] because "in every country and in every age, the priest has been hostile to liberty." Jefferson's "bias against institutionalized Christianity (at about the time he wrote the Declaration) extended to all Protestantism, especially Presbyterianism, as well as Catholicism and Anglicanism."[112] He also rejected the theology of biblical Judaism, though, as Sanford explains, he expressed positive views about the Jewish people:

> The Jews excited Jefferson's sympathy because of the persecution that they had endured, especially because they were "the parent sect and basis of Christendom." Jefferson was proud that America was the first country "to prove that religious freedom is most effectual and to restore to the Jews their social rights," he wrote to the

rabbi of the Jewish synagogue in Savannah, Georgia. The United States, he wrote to John Adams, is an example to "old Europe" and is "destined to be a barrier against the return of ignorance and barbarism." He admitted to another Jewish correspondent, however, that "public opinion needs reformation [of] the prejudices still scowling on your religion."[113]

The Declaration of Independence reflected Jefferson's thinking on these matters. By invoking "the Laws of Nature and of Nature's God" rather than the Judeo-Christian God, it made clear that it was not a Christian document, that it did not reflect uniquely Christian or Judeo-Christian beliefs, and that it was not "a bridge between the Bible and the Constitution." To the contrary, it rejected Christianity, along with other organized religions, as a basis for governance, and it built a wall—rather than a bridge—between the Bible and the Constitution.

In his final letter, on the eve of the fiftieth anniversary of the Declaration of Independence—the day on which both he and John Adams were to die—Jefferson confirmed that this historic document declared our independence not only from British political control but also from European clerical control:

May it [the Declaration of Independence] be to the world, what I believe it will be (to some parts sooner, to others later, but finally to all), the signal of arousing men to burst the chains under which monkish ignorance and superstition had persuaded them to bind themselves, and to assume the blessings and security of self-government. That form which we have substituted, restores the free right to the unbound exercise of reason and freedom of opinion. All eyes are opened, or opening, to the rights of man. The general spread of the light of science has already laid open to every view the palpable truth, that the mass of mankind has not been born with saddles on their backs, nor a favored few booted and spurred, ready to ride them legitimately, by the grace of God.[114]

The last sentence of this letter to Roger C. Weightman was a reference to Jefferson's particular hatred of the apostle Paul, as well as of John Calvin, who preached a "predestinator God" who, in the words of Bolingbroke, "elects some of his creatures to salvation . . . and others to damnation even in the womb of their mothers."[115] Jefferson wrote to John Adams the following:

> I can never join Calvin in addressing his god. He was indeed an atheist, which I can never be; or rather his religion was one of daemonism. If ever man worshipped a false god, he did. The Being described in his 5 points, is not the God whom you and I acknowledge and adore, the Creator and benevolent Governor of the world but a daemon of malignant spirit. It would be more pardonable to believe in no god at all, than to blaspheme Him by the atrocious attributes of Calvin.[116]

Jefferson thus intended his great document of liberty, with its "theology born of 'Nature's God,'" to attack "two claims of absolute authority—that of any government over its subject and that of any religion over the minds of men."[117] Jefferson "saw the concepts of God and man upheld by orthodox theological circles in the colonies as antithetical to the Declaration's theological and political ideals."[118] His own "heterodox theology"—which rejected organized religion in general and the doctrines of orthodox Christianity in particular—"is institutionalized in the Declaration as a primary truth and necessary corollary of its political theory."[119] The Declaration's reliance on human reason and freedom of thought in place of "monkish ignorance and superstition" was indeed a radical departure from the manner by which European nations had governed, with its divine right of kings and its established hierarchical churches.

Many of those who seek to introduce the study of religion into the public schools quote Justice Lewis Powell's concurring opinion in the creationism case in which he said that he would "see no constitutional problem if schoolchildren were taught the nature of the Founding Fathers' religious beliefs and how these beliefs affected the attitudes of the times and the structure of our government."[120] I wonder what Powell's reaction would have been if the antibiblical and anticlerical views of Jefferson and Paine were honestly and fully presented to impressionable young schoolchildren. Indeed, several years ago, in a debate with a representative of the Religious Right who advocated Bible study in elementary school, I proposed—for argument's sake—that *both* the Bible *and* Thomas Paine's *The Age of Reason* be taught together in public schools, to present both sides. There was a nervous silence from my opponent. The last thing most proponents of teaching public school students "about" religion want is honest, objective *teaching*; what they want is exactly the kind of one-sided proselytizing in favor of religion that Jefferson so strongly opposed.

Why, Then, Did the Declaration Invoke God?

Why, then, did an "Enlightenment rationalist," "secular humanist," and "religious skeptic" such as Jefferson invoke God—even Nature's God—in his draft of the Declaration of

Independence? To the early-twenty-first-century reader, who sees all around him disputes between those who support the invocation of God in public declarations and ceremonies and those who oppose it, the inclusion of God in the Declaration of Independence would seem to support the conclusion that Jefferson came down squarely on the side of the former. But to the late-eighteenth-century reader, who saw a very different debate between those who supported organized religion and those who rejected clericalism in favor of free thinking and human reason, Jefferson came down unambiguously on the side of the latter. The Declaration of Independence was a resounding defeat for organized religion in general and traditional Christianity in particular. Indeed, the Declaration, and the godless Constitution as well, were subsequently criticized by influential clergymen who complained of their failure to acknowledge the Christian nature of the United States.[121]

Another challenging question is how Jefferson persuaded his colleagues—first, those on the committee appointed to draft the Declaration, and second, those in the Congress who eventually approved it—to accept his un-Christian and anticlerical reference to "Nature's God" and "Creator" in place of the more orthodox reference to "Almighty God," "Jesus," or even simply "God."

The "Jesus" part of the question is simple. Despite the repeated claims over the years that the United States was founded as a Christian nation, the evidence is clear that the opposite is true. Jefferson strongly opposed "a [proposed] reference to Christ in the Virginia Act Establishing Religious Freedom."[122] Shortly after the issuance of the Declaration and the adoption of the Constitution and the Bill of Rights, President John Adams—who was on the drafting committee of the Declaration—signed a treaty with the Barbary regime of Tripoli, which was ratified by the Senate. That treaty, which is the best contemporaneous evidence, expressly declares that "the government of the United States is not in any sense founded on the Christian religion."[123] This disclaimer followed the view expressed by Roger Williams—the religious leader most responsible for separating church from state in colonial America—more than a century earlier: "No civil state or country can be truly called Christian, although the Christians be in it."[124] It would have been unthinkable for a Declaration drafted by Jefferson, with the approval of Adams and Franklin, to have invoked Jesus or Christianity. Indeed, the word "Christian" appeared only once in Jefferson's original draft: he referred derisively to King George as "the Christian king of Great Britain" who was responsible for the "execrable commerce" in slaves. This entire paragraph was stricken by the Congress.

As to the question of how the deistic, un-Christian reference to Nature's God could have gotten the approval of the drafting committee, it must be recalled that a *majority* of the five-man committee were deists and/or Unitarians—as were many leading colonialists at that time. In fact, Leo Pfeffer lists George Washington, Patrick Henry, George Mason, James Madison, Benjamin Franklin, Thomas Paine, John Adams, and, of course, Thomas Jefferson among the most prominent leaders of the time who were influenced by deism or Unitarianism. Three of those leaders were on the drafting committee, which consisted of Jefferson, John Adams, Benjamin Franklin, Roger Sherman, and Robert R. Livingston.

Washington often referred to the Almighty, but Bishop William White, who knew Washington in Philadelphia and in New York, said, "I do not believe that any degree of recollection will bring to my mind any fact which would prove George Washington to have been a believer in the Christian revelation."[125]

Franklin described himself as "a thorough deist"[126] and "reject[ed] his Christian upbringing."[127] Franklin also was a Freemason who subscribed to the notion of God as "the Great Architect." He supported the ideas of Thomas Paine and "never came to accept the Bible as the divine revelation or Jesus as the son of God."[128] Although he "seldom attended any public worship," he believed in a divinity—probably the same "clockmaker" God of Nature in whom Jefferson believed. "At one point he expressed a belief in a single supreme God who supervised a number of lesser gods, one of whom created our world,"[129] and he "ridiculed the idea that either Adam's sin or the righteousness of Christ could be inherited or 'imputed' to Adam's posterity."[130] There does not appear to be any inconsistency between Franklin's deistic religious beliefs and those reflected in the Declaration. Jon Meacham tells us:

> While Jefferson edited the Gospels, Benjamin Franklin rephrased and rearranged the Book of Common Prayer. Franklin may have rendered the Lord's Prayer into the eighteenth-century vernacular, but his piety had limits: on his first day in Philadelphia as a young man, Franklin recalled falling sound asleep in a Quaker meetinghouse. Many of the Founders were influenced by Deism, an Enlightenment vision of religion, which held that there was a single creator God; some Deists, including Jefferson and Franklin, believed this God worked in the world through providence. For them, Jesus of Nazareth was a great moral teacher—even the greatest in all history— but he was not the Son of God; the Holy Trinity was seen as an invention of a corrupt church more interested in temporal power than in true religion. The mind of man, not the mysteries of the church, was the center of faith.[131]

John Adams, too, questioned traditional religious views throughout his life. As a young man he sided with a controversial Congregationalist minister in his hometown of Braintree, Massachusetts, who rejected Calvinist teachings and preached that the "aim of God was to advance happiness in man." His views were, according to Peter Rinaldo's *Atheists, Agnostics, and Deists in America*, "similar to [those] of the deists in that both believed in the power of reason to establish religious beliefs." Adams's father was dismayed at his son's decision to support such "unorthodox religious views."[132] Adams's legal mentor was a brilliant and prominent local lawyer who believed that "the apostles were nothing more than a company of enthusiasts" who falsely claimed that they performed miracles, and whose word would be thrown out by any court of law. Adams was apparently influenced by these heterodox views. As he later wrote to a friend:

> The Priesthood have in all ancient nations, nearly monopolized learning. . . . And, even since the Reformation, when or where has existed a Protestant or dissenting sect who would tolerate a FREE INQUIRY? The blackest billingsgate, the most ungentlemanly insouciance, the most yahooish brutality is patiently endured, countenanced, propagated and applauded. But touch a solemn truth in collision with the dogma of a sect, though capable of the clearest truth, and you will soon find you have disturbed a nest, and the hornets will swarm about legs and hands and fly into your face and eyes.[133]

In the words of the Adams biographer David McCullough, Adams was repelled by the "spirit of dogmatism and bigotry" he saw in "clergy and laity" alike,[134] just as he was inspired by God's natural wonders and His gift to humans of "reason, to find out the truth." Like Jefferson, he saw "our nobler powers of intelligence and reason" as "the real design and true end of our existence."[135]

Adams agreed with Jefferson in rejecting the doctrine of the Trinity and accepting the "God of nature." He wrote the following to Jefferson in 1815:

> The question before the human race is whether the God of nature shall govern the world by His own laws, or whether priests and kings shall rule it by fictitious miracles? Or, in other words, whether authority is originally in the people? Or whether it has descended for 1800 years in a succession of popes and bishops, or brought down from heaven by the Holy Ghost in the form of a dove in a phial of holy oil.[136]

Adams was critical of traditional Christianity, but he was downright bigoted toward Catholicism. His letters to Jefferson included the following:

> I do not like the reappearance of the Jesuits. . . . Shall we not have regular swarms of them here, in as many disguises as only a king of the gypsies can assume, dressed as printers, publishers, writers and schoolmasters? If ever there was a body of men who merited damnation on earth and in Hell, it is this society of Loyola's. Nevertheless, we are compelled by our system of religious toleration to offer them an asylum.[137]

Adams characterized Catholicism as "fraudulent" and having inflicted "a mortal wound" on Christianity. Finally he asked Jefferson, rhetorically, "Can a free government possibly exist with the Roman Catholic religion?"[138]

Jefferson may not have been correct in predicting that "there is not a young man now living in the United States who will not die an Unitarian,"[139] but apparently he was right about John Adams, who, along with his wife, Abigail, and their son, John Quincy, is buried in a crypt beneath a Unitarian church in Quincy, Massachusetts.

Although John Adams's religious views and practices were somewhat closer to conventional Christianity than Jefferson's and Franklin's, there is no inconsistency between what Adams apparently believed in 1776 and his approval of the deistic language of the Declaration of Independence. Nor can it be argued that Adams was unaware of Jefferson's un-Christian views when Adams approved the language of the Declaration. At about the time the Declaration was written, Adams had chastised Jefferson for "cast[ing] aspersions on Christianity"[140] during a debate over a proposed day of fasting. Adams was reminded of his actions in a subsequent letter from Benjamin Rush:

> You rose and defended the motion, and in reply to Mr. Jefferson's objections to Christianity you said you were sorry to hear such sentiments from a gentleman whom you so highly respected and with whom you agreed upon so many subjects, and that it was the only instance you had ever known of a man of sound sense and real genius that was an enemy to Christianity. You suspected, you told me, that you had offended him, but that he soon convinced you to the contrary by crossing the room and taking a seat in the chair next to you.[141]

Adams knew exactly what he was doing when he signed on to Jefferson's deistic language in the Declaration of Independence.

The religious views of Sherman and Livingston are less well known, though it seems likely that the former was a traditional Christian, while the latter was closer to Jefferson and had expressed religious views that have been characterized as "daring to the point of impiety."[142] In any event, only Jefferson, Franklin, and Adams—among the drafting committee— had any real input into the Declaration's language before it went to the Continental Congress for ratification. The Congress did make several important changes, but it did not tamper with Jefferson's deistic formulation of "Nature's God" and a watchmaking "Creator."[143]

Scholars agree that the debates in Congress over the Declaration are unrecoverable. The transcripts of the Continental Congress recorded neither the debates nor the amendments that were proposed. Only the changes finally adopted give us any evidence of what Congress may have thought of the Declaration as Jefferson submitted it on July 2. Carl Becker states that "since Congress sat, for these debates as a committee of the whole, the Journals give no account of either the debates or the amendments . . . only the form of the Declaration as finally adopted."[144] As the historian Pauline Maier describes it:

> Once again the curtain fell, concealing the delegates as they moved through the document, making changes as they went along, leaving no official record of their proceedings beyond its fruit—the Declaration that, reconstituted as the Continental Congress, they finally adopted. Even the private correspondence of delegates is remarkably silent on what the Committee of the Whole did and why. Only Jefferson's notes on Congress's proceedings discuss the subject in any detail, and Jefferson was anything but a dispassionate observer as the

Committee of the Whole rewrote or chopped off large sections of his draft, eliminating in the end fully a quarter of his text.[145]

In any event, the words of the Declaration were not intended to reflect the ideas of its primary draftsman alone, or even of those members of the Continental Congress who revised and then signed the Declaration. According to the primary craftsman, it was meant to be an "expression of the American mind, and to give that expression the proper tone and spirit called for by the occasion."[146] The "American mind" of the time was willing to accept Jefferson's deistic formulation of the source of rights as a common denominator reflecting the diverse and often heterodox religious views of those who supported independence.

"Nature's God" was a God acceptable to the deists. So, too, was the "Creator" who endowed human beings with "unalienable Rights." Jefferson believed that his watchmaker God had "impressed on the sense of every man" an instinct for certain rights. This is what he wrote to a friend in 1817 about one particular right:

My opinion on the right of Expatriation has been, so long ago as the year 1776, consigned to record in the act of the Virginia code, drawn by myself, recognizing the right expressly, and prescribing the mode of exercising it. The evidence of this natural right, like that of our right to life, liberty, the use of our faculties, the pursuit of happiness, is not left to the feeble and sophistical investigations of reason, but is impressed on the sense of every man. We do not claim these under the charters of kings or legislators, but under the King of kings. If he has made it a law *in* the nature of man to pursue his own happiness, he has left him free in the choice of place as well as mode. [Emphasis added.][147]

The Declaration's reference to the "Supreme Judge of the World," though added by the Congress to the original draft, also was consistent with Jefferson's deistic views of an un-Christian afterlife. He "saw the importance of a belief in eternal judgment for encouraging a moral life of service to society."[148] Jefferson's "Judge," unlike the Christian God, did not reward or punish based on beliefs or acceptance of Jesus. Nor was the afterlife determined by predestination or election. "What really aroused Jefferson's ire was the suggestion that God judged people in the afterlife by their correct belief rather than by their behavior."[149] By agreeing to appeal to the "Supreme Judge of the World," Jefferson was not seeking God's intervention in battle but rather his approval for the good deed of establishing independence.

Finally, the words "Divine Providence," which also were added by Congress, were not inconsistent with Jefferson's nonintervening watchmaker God. In a letter to Benjamin Rush, he wrote about the relationship between Providence and "the order of things": "When great evils happen, I am in the habit of looking out for what good may arise from them as consolations to us, and Providence has in fact so established the order of things, as that most evils are the means of producing some good."[150]

A distinguished student of church-state relations in America, Leo Pfeffer has argued that the framers' references to God in the Declaration of Independence should not be misunderstood to suggest that the framers anticipated—or were willing to accept—that these references be taken to justify practices being championed by the Religious Right today:

It is reasonable to assume that many of the original framers of the document would have opposed the references [to God] if they had anticipated the use to which it was later put. For example, Justice [David J.] Brewer, in *Church of Holy Trinity* v. *United States,* cited the reference to Providence in the Declaration of Independence as one of the items in his long list of religious references and practice to support his conclusion that "this is a *Christian* nation." In view of Jefferson's strong opposition to the maxim that "Christianity is part of the common law," and to a reference to Christ in the Virginia Act Establishing Religious Freedom, it is quite unlikely that he would have approved this use by Justice Brewer of the reference to Providence in the Declaration of Independence.[151]

The un-Christian Declaration of Independence was followed eleven years later by what Isaac Kramnick and R. Laurence Moore have aptly called "the godless Constitution," in which God is never invoked and religion is mentioned but once, in the provision that "no religious test shall ever be required as a qualification to any office or public trust under the United States."[152] Yet the parochial partisans of the Religious Right who deliberately misread history in an effort to turn the Declaration into a Christian document do the same with the Constitution. As the founder of the Religious Right's Rutherford Institute said: "The entire Constitution was written to promote a Christian order."[153] Pat Robertson, Ralph Reed, James Dobson, and others have echoed this ahistoric fallacy.

The truth, according to the historians Kramnick and Moore, is that "Americans, in the era of the Revolution, were a distinctly unchurched people. The highest estimates for the late eighteenth century make only about 10 to 15 percent of the population church members."[154] As Hector St. John de Crevecoeur reported: "Religious indifference is imperceptibly disseminated from one end of the continent to the other."[155] According to historians of that era, "churches would have been almost completely empty had it not been for women."[156] And considering the low status of women in those days, particularly with regard to politics, from which they were virtually excluded, it is fair to conclude that the churches did not have much of an impact on the Declaration, the Constitution, or other important political documents or actions of that period.

This is not to say that Americans were atheists, irreligious, or godless. "In a general way most of them were Christians," according to Kramnick and Moore, but "Americans in 1776 had a long way to go before making themselves strongly Christian or strongly anything else relating to a religious persuasion."[157] As Carl Becker observed, the "natural order" and non-Christian deistic theologies reflected in Jefferson's draft of the Declaration "were the accepted premises, the preconceptions of most eighteenth-century thinkers, not only in America, but also in England and France."[158] Even Alexis de Tocqueville, who is frequently quoted by the Religious Right to prove that nineteenth-century Americans were quite religious, argued that religion should not—and in America did not—involve itself in political parties or political controversies. Americans then, in truth, were far less traditionally religious, far less likely to belong to churches, and far, far less influenced in their politics by religious leaders than they are today.

Conclusion

What, then, can be fairly concluded from this history? Despite its references to "Nature's God," "Creator," "Supreme Judge," and "Divine Providence," the Declaration of Independence was a document designed to "burst the chains" with which organized religion—especially orthodox Christianity—had shackled previous governments. It was an anticlerical document that elevated nature, science, and human reason over "monkish ignorance and superstition." It represented a defeat for churches, clergymen, and faith, and a victory for "the rights of man," for the separation of church from state, and for reason. It marked the beginning of the end of the religious state and the emergence of the secular state based on the consent of the governed, rather than the revealed word of God. If they had been alive at the time, Falwell, Robertson, Dobson, and Keyes would surely have opposed it and joined with those who subsequently tried, and failed, to declare America to be a Christian nation ruled by "the Lord Jesus Christ."

According to Leo Pfeffer, attempts to constitutionalize or legislate the Christian God into our legal system have persisted throughout our history:

> Omission of reference to God or Christ in the Constitution was bitterly criticized by some during the debates in the states during its ratification. Indeed, two Presbyterian church groups resolved not to vote at elections until the Constitution should be amended to acknowledge the sovereignty of God and Christ. Others decided on more practical measures. In 1863 representatives from eleven Protestant denominations organized the National Reform Association, one of whose principal purposes was "to secure such an amendment to the Constitution of the United States as will declare the nation's allegiance to Jesus Christ and its acceptance of the moral laws of the Christian religion, and so indicate that this is a Christian nation, and place all the Christian laws,

institutions, and usages of our government on an unde-
niably legal basis in the fundamental law of the land."

Accordingly, the next year the Association formally petitioned Congress to amend the preamble of the Constitution
as to read

We, the People of the United States, *humbly acknowledg-
ing Almighty God as the source of all authority and power
in the civil government, the Lord Jesus Christ as the Ruler
among the nations, His revealed will as the supreme law of
the land, in order to constitute a Christian government,*
and in order to form a more perfect Union, establish justice, insure domestic Tranquility, provide for the common
defence, promote the general Welfare, *and secure the
inalienable rights and the blessings of life, liberty, and the
pursuit of happiness to ourselves, our posterity, and all the
people,* do ordain and establish this Constitution for the
United States of America. [Emphasis added.]

As late as February 1951, Senator Ralph Flanders of Vermont introduced a proposal to amend the Constitution to add
an article reading:

Section 1. This nation devoutly recognizes the authority and law of Jesus Christ, Saviour and Ruler of nations
through whom are bestowed the blessings of Almighty
God.[159]

Every such effort has failed. Yet those who today seek
to Christianize America now—falsely—claim that the
Declaration supports their very un-Jeffersonian vision of a
Christian America based on the divinity of Jesus and the
authority of the Bible. The language of the Declaration was as

unbiblical and un-Christian as could achieve the level of consensus required to serve its purposes—it is close to the theology that got Spinoza excommunicated from Judaism. It distorts the historical record and insults the memory of those who drafted the Declaration to believe that Jefferson, Franklin, and Adams would have anything in common with today's evangelical Christian fundamentalists who invoke their names while rejecting the findings of science—including those of Darwin and Einstein—because they appear to conflict with a literal reading of the Bible. Jefferson, Franklin, and Adams would be turning in their graves if they knew how their views were being misused by today's Religious Right.

Jon Meacham summarizes the history in the following nuanced manner:

> The nation's public religion, then, holds that there is a God, the one Jefferson called the "Creator" and "Nature's God" in the Declaration of Independence. The God of public religion made all human beings in his image and endowed them, as Jefferson wrote, with sacred rights to life, liberty, and the pursuit of happiness. What the God of public religion has given, no king, no president, no government can abridge—hence the sanctity of human rights in America. The God of public religion is interested in the affairs of the world. The God of public religion may be seen as capable of rewarding or punishing individuals or the nation either here and now or later, beyond time. And the God of public religion is sometimes spoken of as a God bound to the American nation, in Jefferson's words, "as Israel of old."
>
> Properly understood, the God of public religion is not the God of Abraham or God the Father of the Holy Trinity. The Founding Fathers had ample opportunity to

use Christian imagery and language in the Declaration of Independence and Constitution, but did not. At the same time, they were not absolute secularists. They wanted God in American public life, but, given the memory of religious warfare that could engulf and destroy whole governments, they saw the wisdom in distinguishing between private and public religion. In churches and in homes, anyone could believe and practice what he wished. In public business of the nation, however, it was important to the Founders to speak of God in a way that was unifying, not divisive. "Nature's God" was the path they chose, and it has served the nation admirably. Despite generations of subsequent efforts to amend the Constitution to include Jesus or to declare that America is a "Christian nation," no president across three centuries has made an even remotely serious attempt to do so.[160]

It is important that today's secularists not engage in a mirror-image distortion of what the Religious Right is now seeking to do. It would be wrong to conclude that the Declaration of Independence supports the entire agenda of those who would remove all references to God from public pronouncements. Although that would be my own strong personal preference, I cannot find support for it in the history or text of the Declaration. The Declaration was drafted at a different time in our history, when our population was far more homogeneous—especially with regard to religion. Almost everyone in the colonies was a Protestant of some sort, at least nominally, and believed in some kind of God. The contentious issues of the day were different from those of our own. Whether generic references to "God" might be deemed offensive to some atheists, agnostics, separationists, or adherents to nontheistic religions was not a pressing issue. It is impossible to know for certain what its drafters and ratifiers would say about all of today's diverse church-state issues if they were living in today's very different world. Contentious special pleaders can find snippets of writings that can be cited in support of, and in opposition to, the agendas of each side, especially in the numerous letters written over so long a period by the likes of Jefferson, Adams, and Franklin. What can be said, with some degree of confidence, on the basis of a fair reading of the relevant record, is that the Declaration's primary drafters—though they believed in God—would not be on the side of those who would govern by religious authority and biblical revelation rather than by principles of democracy and reason.

To dramatize this point, I have gathered various questions sent to candidates by groups representative of the current Religious Right. These questions are designed to determine whether these candidates, who seek the endorsement of the Religious Right, pass various "litmus tests." Those who respond—and some who do not—are given scores and these scores are then released to the public. It will be revealing to see how Thomas Jefferson would have scored on these tests. As I have previously noted, it is impossible to know for certain how eighteenth- or nineteenth-century politicians would answer every question about current issues, but we can be very close to certain on those issues about which Jefferson felt strongly and left a substantial written record.

Virtually every litmus test asks about religious practices in public schools. We know that Jefferson was adamantly opposed to teaching the Bible to schoolchildren and to public prayers in schools.

The test also asks about the teaching of evolution and creationism. We can be relatively certain how Jefferson would have responded to these issues if he were alive today, based on what I have shown he believed. He thought that the biblical story of creation was an ignorant human contrivance, and although he lived before Darwin, he corresponded extensively with scientists about fossils, extinction, and other issues of paleontology. His beliefs were based on the findings of science, not the revelations in the Bible. He surely would have favored the teaching of scientific evolution, not biblical creationism. But what about "scientific" creationism that purports to rely not on biblical accounts but rather on the findings of science? Here we can be less certain. In one respect, Jefferson can be characterized as a nonbiblical, scientific creationist. He believed that the God of Nature had created human beings (as well as the rules of human and physical nature). This belief was based on his understanding of science. The difference between Jefferson and most contemporary religious creationists is that Jefferson was willing to be proved wrong by science, whereas most of today's creationists generally use— misuse—science to confirm what they already "know" to be true, because the Bible says so. If Jefferson was convinced, as is the deeply religious Professor Stephen Carter, that creationism is "bad science,"[161] he would reject it, as Carter does. But in Jefferson's day, proof of God's creation "by design" seemed like good science, and Jefferson accepted it. I don't know whether he would accept it today.

Another question is about the governmental funding of religious schools. Jefferson was adamantly opposed to the government compelling anyone, through taxation, to support religion, even one's own religion. He called it "sinful and tyrannical" to require "a man to furnish contributions of money for the propagation of opinions which he disbelieves," and wrong to force him even to support "this or that teacher of his own religious persuasion," unless he chose to make a contribution.[162] Jefferson would almost certainly oppose current efforts to divert taxpayer money to religious schools.

Yet another question asks whether the candidate would, if elected president, place a Nativity scene on the lawn of the White House. Jefferson, who did not believe in the virgin birth or any of the other alleged miracles surrounding the birth of the very human Jesus, would not have approved of crèches, but even if he did, he would be opposed to governmental displays of peculiarly Christian symbols.

Another common question revolves around the invocation of God on coins, in the Pledge of Allegiance, and in other ceremonial settings. Jefferson himself invoked God in the Declaration and even in his bill for establishing religious freedom in Virginia. But so did Thomas Paine and other more radical anti-Christians. Invoking God was simply not controversial in Jefferson's day, because to Jefferson it meant "Nature's God," not the Bible's God. It is impossible to know what Jefferson would think today, when invoking God is quite controversial and divisive, because it tends to mean the Judeo-Christian God of the Bible. To lean over backward, I will say that Jefferson might have received a positive score from the Religious Right on this question.

He probably would not have been in favor of abolishing, as the Religious right is, the Department of Education, the National Endowment for the Arts and Humanities, or the Office of Surgeon General, since he was so supportive of education, science, medicine, philosophy, and the arts, though he was wary of federal involvement in matters left, by the Constitution, to the states.

Other questions deal with abortion, homosexuality, pornography, assisted suicide, and stem cell research to cure diseases. There are simply insufficient data to know what Jefferson would say about abortion. He appeared to favor the criminalization of homosexuality. His views on free speech probably would have placed him on the side of those who oppose governmental censorship, even of pornography, though that is not certain. He was sympathetic to suicide. And he believed in the progress of science to cure illness.

All in all, it is fair to conclude that Thomas Jefferson would have scored quite low—certainly less than 25 percent—on any Religious Right litmus test. He probably would have scored somewhere between Barney Frank and Bill Clinton. Jefferson surely would not have received the endorsement of the Religious Right for president based on his answers to their litmus test questions. Yet they now fraudulently claim his posthumous endorsement for their efforts to tear down the wall of separation between church and state, which was among his most enduring contributions to American constitutional theory and practice.

The out-of-context quotation of Jefferson that appears on his memorial in Washington, when placed back into its proper context, perhaps best summarizes Jefferson's views regarding God, on the one hand, and organized religion, on the other. The quote on the memorial invokes God: "I have sworn upon the altar of God, eternal hostility against every form of tyranny over the mind of man."[163]

These words were selected in 1943, according to Kramnick and Moore, to convey America's "enduring commitment, as a religious people, to oppose vigilantly political oppression and tyranny in all forms—be it that of George III, German Kaisers, Hitler or Japanese aggressors."[164] But when Jefferson wrote these words, in 1800, in the midst of his campaign for president, he directed them at the tyranny of the *clergy*. Benjamin Rush, a close friend and fellow religious skeptic, had written to Jefferson that the clergy were attacking him with claims that his election would undermine their preeminent position in American life. Jefferson's reply reads in relevant part as follows:

> I promised you a letter on Christianity, which I have not forgotten. On the contrary, it is because I have reflected on it, that I find much more time necessary for it than I can at present dispose of. I have a view of the subject which ought to displease neither the rational Christian nor Deists, and would reconcile many to a character they have too hastily rejected. I do not know that it would reconcile the *genus irritable vatum* [the irritable tribe of priests] who are all in arms against me. Their hostility is on too interesting ground to be softened. . . . The successful experiment made under the prevalence of that delusion on the clause of the Constitution, which, while it secured the freedom of the press, covered also the freedom of religion, had given to the clergy a very favorite hope of obtaining an establishment of a particular form of Christianity through the United States; and as every sect believes its own form the true one, every one perhaps hoped for his own, but especially the Episcopalians and Congregationalists. The returning good sense of our country threatens abortion to their hopes, and they believe that any portion of power confided to me, will be exerted in opposition to their schemes. And they believe rightly: for I have sworn upon the altar of God, eternal hostility against every form of tyranny over the mind of man. But this is all they have to fear from me; and enough too in their opinion.[165]

The man who drafted the Declaration of Independence was a man willing to invoke his God—the God of Nature—

against organized churches and irritable clerics who would impose "tyranny over the mind of man" by establishing their religious doctrines—or any religious doctrine—as the only truth. As Kramnick and Moore summarized it: "Jefferson was not a godless man or intrinsically irreligious. While committed to the strict separation of church and state, to a godless politics, and thus fiercely anticlerical, he was also a man of deeply felt *private* religious conviction."[166]

It is this distinction between *private beliefs* and *public politics*—a distinction central to Jefferson and many of his contemporaries—that is ignored, even distorted, by today's public panderers of the Religious Right, who miscite the Declaration in support of their parochial causes—to borrow an apt phrase from Carl Becker—"without fear and without research."

John T. Noonan Jr., a federal judge and a deeply religious man, well summarized the creed of many of the founders of the Declaration and the Constitution when he reminded us that "nations do not worship, persons do."[167] Our Declaration of Independence may well have become, as one historian called it, "American scripture," but to its author it was secular scripture.

2

The Christian Right's Strategy to Turn the Declaration into a Baptismal Certificate

The strategy of the current crusade by the Religious Right to Christianize America envisages a two-step process: The first requires a lowering of the wall of separation between church and state to a level that would permit the introduction of generic religion—God, nonsectarian prayer, multiple religious images—into the governmental sphere; once this is accomplished the next step would be to insist that America's true religion is Christianity, since our nation was founded by Christians on Christian principles.

The first step, which sounds benign to many but is seen by the Religious Right as a Trojan horse hiding an army of Christian soldiers, is now becoming mainstream and is likely to be approved, in general terms, by the current Supreme Court. The second step is still the province of the extreme Religious Right, but that group is growing in size and influence, and its goal of a Christian America, with other religions being tolerated as "second class" and atheism and agnosticism being condemned as immoral, is no longer merely a prayer.

Moreover, experience suggests that once religion, even generic religion, becomes sufficiently entwined in governance, it is only a matter of time before a competition ensues as to which is the true religion of our nation. Jacob Henry, a Jew who was elected to North Carolina's legislature in 1808 but was blocked from taking his seat by a law requiring him to accept the divinity of the New Testament, posed the following rhetorical question: "Will you drive from your shores and from the shelter of your constitution all who do not lay their oblations on the same altar, observe the same ritual, and subscribe to the same dogmas? If so, which among the various sects into which we are divided shall be the favored one?"[1]

As if to demonstrate that intolerance once practiced *against* Jews can also be practiced *by* some Jews against other minorities, a Jewish right-wing talk show host named Dennis Prager led a campaign to disallow the first Muslim elected to congress (in November 2006) to take an oath of office on the Koran. Prager insisted that congressman Keith Ellison

> should not be allowed to do so—not because of any American hostility to the Koran, but because the act undermines American civilization. Insofar as a member of Congress taking an oath to serve America and uphold its values is concerned, America is interested in only one book, the Bible. If you are incapable of taking an oath on that book, don't serve in Congress.[2]

Prager's bigotry was immediately condemned by Jewish organizations across the ideological spectrum. This is what the Anti-Defamation League of B'nai Brith said:

Prager is flat-out wrong when he asserts that Representative Ellison's use of a Koran would be "damaging to the fabric of American civilization." To the contrary, the U.S. Constitution guarantees that "no religious test shall ever be required" to hold public office in America. Members of Congress, like all Americans, should be free to observe their own religious practices without government interference or coercion.

Prager's patriotic prattling is misinformed on the facts, too. No Member of Congress is officially sworn in with a Bible. Under House rules, the official swearing-in ceremony is done in the House chambers, with the Speaker of the House administering the oath of office en masse. No Bibles or other holy books are used at all. Members may, if they choose, also have a private ceremony with family and friends. At these unofficial ceremonies, Members frequently solemnize the event by taking an oath while holding a personal family Bible.

Prager ridiculously asserts that permitting Rep. Ellison to take the oath of office would "be doing more damage to the unity of America and to the value system that has formed this country than the terrorists of 9-11." What he fails to understand is that what truly unifies all Americans is a value system built on religious freedom and pluralism, not dogmatism and coercion.

Prager presents intolerant, ugly views. His comparison of Ellison's desire to "choose his favorite book" to that of the right of a racist elected to public office to use Hitler's *Mein Kampf* is outrageous.[3]

Not to be outdone, former Alabama chief justice Roy Moore, who was removed from the bench for refusing to obey a federal court order to remove a monument featuring the

Ten Commandments from the Alabama Supreme Court building, said the following:

> Enough evidence exists for Congress to question Ellison's qualifications to be a member of Congress as well as his commitment to the Constitution in view of his apparent determination to embrace the Quran and an Islamic philosophy directly contrary to the principles of the Constitution. But common sense alone dictates that in the midst of a war with Islamic terrorists we should not place someone in a position of great power who shares their doctrine. In 1943, we would never have allowed a member of Congress to take their oath on "Mein Kampf," or someone in the 1950s to swear allegiance to the "Communist Manifesto." Congress has the authority and should act to prohibit Ellison from taking the congressional oath today![4]

To cap it off, a congressman has actually said that he would disallow Ellison from taking his seat because of his request to swear in on the Koran. According to the *New York Times*, Representative Virgil H. Goode Jr. (R-Virginia), in a letter to his constituents, said that voters must "wake up" or else there will "likely be many more Muslims elected to office and demanding the use of the Koran."[5] Of course Congressman Ellison was allowed to take the oath of office. The question should be whether Congressman Goode should be allowed to take his oath and sit in his elected office. He has, after all, violated his oath of office, in which he promised to "support and defend the Constitution of the United States," which intentionally and emphatically prohibits any and all religious tests.

In the end, Congressman Ellison took his private oath on the Koran. The particular Koran he chose was the one owned by none other than Thomas Jefferson. The Ellison episode demonstrates how the introduction of religion into governmental activities can sow the seeds of religious intolerance.

This book demonstrates that the Religious Right's reliance on the Declaration of Independence is misplaced. The entire thrust of the Declaration is the opposite of how the Religious Right is now characterizing it. The Declaration represented the triumph of reason over religious dogma. It is not "[a] declaration of dependence on God."[6] In any event, the God of the Declaration was not the God of the Bible, the Lord of Hosts, the Father of Jesus. He was neither the Jewish God of the Old Testament, nor the Christian God of the New Testament. As Jon Meacham put it, "[T]he God [Jefferson] wrote of was in no explicit way the God of Abraham, much less the Father of the Holy Trinity."[7] He was "Nature's God"—the God for whom Spinoza was excommunicated from the Amsterdam Jewish community; the God for whom Jefferson was condemned as anti-Christian; the God in whom the virulently anti-Christian Thomas Paine believed. Nor was the Declaration based on the Bible, a book so despised by Jefferson—he believed the New Testament was written by "ignorant unlettered men" and the Old Testament was riddled with draconian laws imposed by a vengeful God—that he took razor and paste to it and created his own version, shorn of miracles, the supernatural, and the divinity of Jesus. (For this, he was called a non-Christian and his writings were banned in parts of the United States.)

The most important founders of our great nation—Washington, Adams, Jefferson, and Madison—were deists. So were Franklin, Paine, and Hamilton.[8] And "Christian deist" is an oxymoron.[9] Jonathan Edwards described deists as anti-Christians who had wholly cast off the Christian religion, and are professed infidels. They are not like the Heretics, Arians, Socinians, and others, who own the Scriptures to be the word of God, and hold the Christian religion to be the true religion, but only deny these and these fundamental doctrines of the Christian religion; they deny the whole Christian religion. Indeed they own the being of a God; but they deny that Christ was the son of God, and say he was a mere cheat; and so they say all the prophets and apostles were; and they deny the whole Scripture. They deny that any of it is the word of God. They deny any revealed religion, or any word of God at all; and say that God has given mankind no other light to walk by but their own reason.[10]

It is civil blasphemy and intellectual heresy—to say nothing of chutzpah—for the Religious Right to turn the words of the authors of the Declaration on their heads and seek to use them as a justification for converting the United States into precisely the opposite of what the founders intended. But that is what the Religious Right is doing today. Listen to their own words and then compare them to the beliefs of those who wrote our Declaration of Independence.

What the Religious Right Is Saying about the Declaration

The Reverend Jerry Falwell, the founder of the Moral Majority and now the leader of its successor, the Liberty Foundation, and the founder of Liberty University, has written that "any diligent student of American history finds that our great nation was founded by godly men upon godly principles to be a Christian nation." He goes on to say:

The Founders actually included their Christian beliefs in their Declaration of Independence. What did they believe?

- They believed in a Creator.

- They believed God created them in His own image.

- They believed that God's supernatural act to create mankind should continue to be extended to every person, which is clearly implied when they wrote "they are endowed by their Creator with certain unalienable rights, that among these are life, liberty and the pursuit of happiness." It is not a stretch to believe that their use of the word "life" implied born and unborn life, black and white life, life for all humans.

- They believed in absolute truth which they called unalienable rights or self-evident truths. The Founders were men of the Bible. They considered this "absolute Truth . . . self-evident Truths."

Similarly, the televangelist and onetime presidential candidate Pat Robertson has characterized our original documents of liberty as designed for "self-government by Christian people." On the basis of this history, he hopes that we will recognize that Jesus "is Lord of the government, and the church, and business and education, and hopefully, one day, Lord of the press. I see Him involved in everything."

Dr. James Dobson, the head of the conservative group Focus on the Family and a leader of the Religious Right, has observed, "Given this vast volume of historical evidence, it is utterly foolish to deny that we have been, from the beginning, a people of faith whose government is built wholly on a Judeo-Christian foundation. Yet those of our people who do not study history can be duped into believing anything."

Likewise, the Coral Ridge Ministries, an Evangelical group dedicated to "protecting America's Christian heritage by encouraging the application of biblical principles to all spheres of our culture," distributes glossy pamphlets featuring the Declaration of Independence, along with the message that "antivirtue advocates" who want to remove God and Christianity from public life "have wandered far from the original intent of our founding fathers."

Former vice-presidential candidate and senator Joseph Lieberman also believes that we are a faith-based nation, citing the Declaration: "Our rights to life, liberty and the pursuit of happiness [are] based on what our Creator, God, gave us, creating each of us in the image of God." (It is the Bible, however, and not the Declaration, that says we are created "in the image of God.") And former president George H. W. Bush has said that unless a person believes in the God of the Declaration of Independence, he cannot be a true American. This false association between religion and patriotism endangers the very principles of both the Declaration, which mandates equality, and the Constitution, which guarantees that "no religious test" shall ever be imposed for officeholding, and presumably for citizenship in the United States. It also threatens the wall of separation erected by the First Amendment, despite the parochial claim by some that the First Amendment was proposed as a "way to encourage the influence of religious belief on people."[11]

Nor is this perverse view of the Declaration limited to preachers and politicians. Serious scholars such as Professor Michael Novak have made similar claims. In his 1999 Francis Boyer Lecture, Novak argued that the God of Jefferson's Declaration "is not, and cannot be, a remote watchmaker God." Rather, it is the God of the Bible—the God who "chooses 'chosen' peoples and 'almost chosen peoples'" and "who plays favorites." Novak's biblical God of the Declaration regards us all as fallen "sinners." And Novak apparently believes that Jefferson agreed with the eminent British jurist Sir William Blackstone that "the Law of Moses" is "the font and spring of constitutional government." Novak goes even further in claiming that by using the words "Creator" and "Nature's God," Jefferson twice referred to God "*in Biblical terms*" (emphasis added). Finally, in his most insulting misstatement, he asserts that among the important principles enshrined in the Declaration is one that denies there can be a "republic," "liberty," or "virtue" "without religion."

Anson Phelps Stoke, the author of a three-volume study of church and state in America, published in 1950, argues that Christian values "permeate" the Declaration of Independence. "The ideal of the Declaration is of course a definitely Christian one," especially when "considered along with the references to the Deity." He believes the Declaration is based on "fundamental Christian teachings," including "our duties toward God."

Judge Andrew Napolitano, the senior judicial analyst for the Fox News Channel, said on *The Big Story with John Gibson*, "in America, as we all know from basic high school social studies, we have a Constitution and a Declaration of Independence that embodies Judeo-Christian moral values."[12]

Gary Amos and Richard Gardiner, in their book *Never Before in History*, write:

> The Declaration is not simply a product of Deism, the Enlightenment, the Renaissance, or Graeco-Roman philosophy. This is not to say that these sources did not play a role in America's founding—they did. But if we look closely at the wording and the ideas contained in the Declaration, it becomes clear that the primary influence

that shaped the document was the Christian tradition in law and theology.

It is no contradiction to say that Jefferson adopted a Christian view of law and rights even though he himself was not a Christian in the traditional sense. Jefferson was immersed in a Christian culture. Whether he personally acknowledged Christ as Savior matters little to whether his theories were Christian. Jefferson absorbed, by cultural osmosis, the general worldview of his Christian mentors.

Jefferson's cultural context was thoroughly Christian.[13]

An article posted on RaceMatters.org falsely asserts that "52 of the 55 signers of the Declaration of Independence were orthodox, deeply committed Christians . . . [and] [t]he other three all believed in the Bible as the divine truth, the God of the scripture, and His personal intervention."[14]

University of South Dakota School of Law Associate Professor Patrick M. Garry, in testimony before the House Judiciary Committee regarding legal propriety of the public/governmental expression of religion in America, testified that "the framers [did] not believe in a wall of separation between church and state," and that "[t]he separationist approach contradicts the intentions of the First Amendment framers, who never intended the notion of separation to justify discrimination against religion's role in the public sphere." Garry quoted Justice Douglas's proposition that "[w]hen the state encourages religious instruction or cooperates with religious authorities . . . it follows the best of our traditions." He later asserted that "[r]eligious beliefs found frequent expression in the acts and proceedings of early American legislative bodies," pointing to the "five references to God [that] appear in the Declaration of Independence" as evidence supportive of his views.[15]

Senator James Inhofe (R-Oklahoma), in response to the

question of whether he "would vote to confirm an atheist to the Supreme Court," answered as follows:

> No, I would not. To me, that totally contradicts everything that this country is founded on—including our Constitution, including our original oaths of office. Back in the colonial days, the whole purpose that people came here and lost their lives was to achieve the freedoms, of which the major freedom is freedom to love your Lord.[16]

In other words, this senator, who took an oath to support the Constitution, has said he would violate the explicit command of Article VI, Section 3, of the Constitution that "no religious test shall ever be required as a qualification to any office or public trust under the United States." Moreover, such a refusal to confirm an agnostic or atheist nominee would have kept the great Justice Oliver Wendell Holmes Jr. off the Court, as well as, perhaps, Justices Felix Frankfurter and Benjamin Cardozo. And who knows how many other justices, including some currently serving, harbor their own private doubts about religion? Presidential candidate Mitt Romney would also impose a religious test for the presidency of the United States, saying on February 19, 2007, that "we need to have a person of faith lead the country," thus excluding Jefferson and probably Lincoln.

The Declaration "Curriculum": An Effort to Smuggle Religion into the Public Schools

Among the most insidious misuses of the Declaration by elements of the Religious Right has been their subtle efforts to devise a curriculum for impressionable schoolchildren that teaches—preaches? proselytizes? propagandizes?—that the authors of the Declaration intended it to provide a biblical basis for our nation's governance. The Declaration, so understood, or perhaps misunderstood, becomes the basis for teaching biblical creationism, opposition to abortion and homosexuality, and the immorality of atheism, agnosticism, and free thinking.

During his 1996 presidential campaign, Alan Keyes, who was running for the Republican nomination, argued that the authors of the Declaration of Independence intended it to be a "bridge between the Bible and the Constitution—between the basis of our moral faith and the basis of our political life." Keyes agreed with former president George H. W. Bush that unless a person believes in the God of the Declaration of Independence, he cannot be a true American. Keyes also has said that the God of the Declaration—"Nature's God"—is not "some mechanistic deity of nature." Rather, it is "a very biblical God," a "very personal God."

Keyes started a group called the Declaration Foundation, whose mission includes the "development of a Declaration curriculum" for use in private and eventually public schools (which he calls "government schools"). The goal of this curriculum would be to persuade schoolchildren that the Declaration of Independence is not based on principles of democracy but rather on the word of God, as revealed by the Bible. He claims that the principles of the Declaration—particularly the references to "creator" and "created"—favor the teaching of *biblical* creationism, which he characterizes as "not religious" but "American." He believes that these principles also support prayer in public schools, while they oppose homosexuality, abortion, and atheism.

Keyes also has complained "that I just want to explain to my son Andrew what the Declaration says," namely that by referring to a Creator, it supports *biblical* creationism. He then goes on to assert: "How dare you stop me," suggesting that anyone in America would try to stop a parent, as distinguished from a public school teacher, from telling his son about creationism.

Shortly thereafter, Richard Ferrier and Andrew Seeley, two teachers at the small Catholic school Thomas Aquinas College,[17] working in tandem with Keyes, published a curriculum titled *Declaration Statesmanship: A Course in American Government*. Now in its third edition (2006), this curriculum purports to teach the history of the Declaration in an objective manner, but a close reading of its contents reveals its real purpose: to proselytize the students who study it to accept the entirely ahistorical view of the Declaration as America's baptismal certificate.

The curriculum's underlying premise is that the authors of the Declaration believed that without organized religion, as taught in the churches, there can be no morality, liberty, or democracy. This theme, echoed by Keyes, recurs throughout the Declaration curriculum. The founding generation, according to this view, "knew from experience that strong religious faith was essential to free institutions" (pages 143–44). They selectively quote, often out of context, early American statesmen, conflating belief in "Nature's God" with its opposite, namely belief in the Bible's God. They miscite Jefferson and Franklin—both deists—as believing that the "moral teaching" of the Bible "was the most enlightened ever developed" (page 13), though at another point they refer to "Jefferson's hostility to theological and scriptural studies" (page 14). They claim that the idea of natural rights comes from "two different sources": The first was "the political philosophy of a number of English and French writers." "The other, *undoubtedly more important*, source was the Bible" (page 13, emphasis added).

"We are free," the authors of this curriculum argue, only because "we are made in the image of the all-wise God, and we have a bit of His light in our minds, and by that bit we strive to live according to His laws, 'the laws of nature and of nature's God'" (page 103). (They deliberately do not capitalize *nature* as the author of the Declaration did, but only *God*.)

The authors also cite Lincoln, a man who was accused of being "a scoffer at religion" (page 120) and who, according to Jon Meacham, "never joined a church,"[18] as "preaching [a] political religion" (page 103). Lincoln, in fact, condemned those who misused the Declaration of Independence to further an agenda inconsistent with its values—in that case the continuing "bondage of the negro." Lincoln complained that the Declaration "is assaulted, and sneered at, and torn, till, if its framers could rise from their graves, they could not at all recognize it" (page 107). The same could be said about the authors of the Declaration curriculum and others who distort the Declaration so as to make it appear to be a prescription for theocratic government based on the Bible, as interpreted by its most reactionary believers.

Just listen to the bottom-line conclusion, the "commercial," as it were, of the Declaration curriculum, as it rails against secular efforts to "undermine marriage and the family." Its attack is directed—sometimes subtly, other times overtly—against gay marriage, abortion, premarital sex, and our "Godless" nation, all in the name of the Declaration of Independence:

> Today, the marriage-based two-parent family is under stress as never before. Our tax laws and social legislation encourage mothers to hand over the care of children to governmental agencies, our divorce rates are much higher than in the past, the police have their hands full tracking down "deadbeat dads," illegitimate births are at

shockingly high levels, and the very notion of a normal family, consisting of two adults, *a man and a woman* united in marriage, and their children, is questioned. . . . Even "value-free" sociological research confirms that children raised outside the marriage-based, two-parent family have worse chances in life, greater incidence of crime and drug addiction, lower grades in school, higher rates of poverty and disease.

"For better or worse, for richer and poorer, in sickness and in health, till death do you part." . . . This is what the marital commitment means. It is sealed by a vow made to God. Only if we believe in the possibility and nobility of self-control can we even contemplate such a vow. Only if freedom exists, can marriage come to be. And only if we can take responsibility for our own choices can marriage survive.

There is an evil spirit abroad today (it often comes to us through the airwaves, on television and radio) that whispers to us, "the marital commitment doesn't mean much. *You don't have to wait for marriage to enjoy sex. If an inconvenient child is conceived, you may destroy it in the womb.* If you are unhappy in your marriage, you should be free to abandon spouse and children to find your own personal fulfillment." . . .

Tocqueville thought that there would never be a people both free and irreligious. We may wonder whether there can long be a people politically free and at the same time indifferent to marriage and careless of innocent children [page151–152]. . . .

We have said that *religious worship* has always been the keystone of the arch of the American republic. Over the last forty years, however, God has been exiled from our public life. He can't be supplicated in public schools. He can't be honored in public displays. He is generally unwelcome in our movies and TV shows, except those that mock the simple or hypocritical people who worship Him. It used to be a sign of character, or at least of propriety, when a political official submitted his actions to the judgment of a higher being; now, in some circles, it is a cause of suspicion if a public man admits he prays.

Moral revolutions do not stand still. Thus we see that first comes an attack on moral restraint to preserve freedom wrongly understood, and then soon after comes, in excuse for immorality, the denial that there can be freedom at all. Likewise, some begin by denying God so that man may be properly exalted. Man, they think, cannot be the greatest being, if there is God. Is man not free, autonomous, unbounded by law or limit or even condition? Yet soon it happens that *they deny that man has any soul*, for the soul knows it did not make itself and desires to know more than itself. In order that man not have such immortal aspirations, which point beyond himself, *he must be conceived soulless, a random swarm of atomic particles, without spirit, or will, or finally, freedom.* Thus, caught up in the revolution, a few years ago, a federal court ordered Louisiana public schools to cease using abstinence-only sex education program because it violated the separation of church and state by teaching that man is more than a beast!

Although the attack on the public role of religion opened with a handful of specific Supreme Court decisions, it now reaches deeply into the public mind. Even some pious Americans think that any public decision that conforms with a religious teaching might be un-American. If some judge, teacher, or public official cries out "violation of the First Amendment," many good Americans are at a loss how to answer him.

We Americans today sense that something is wrong, deeply wrong. . . . Faced with the promotion of these evils, we are speechless, incapable of giving reasons, silent, and ashamed of our silence, but not, of course, contented. But we are not altogether lost as a people. We have only to recall what made us a people, and to make it shine in our speech, in our deeds, and in all our lives.

In order to become worthy of our freedom, worthy of our national might, and worthy of the burden of responsibility that that surpassing might places upon us, in a world filled with the poor, the vulnerable, and the innocent, we need only once again live by the Declaration of Independence. [Emphasis added.]

Not surprisingly, the curriculum ends with a sermon by Alan Keyes, about human equality "under God," to which the students are told to respond as follows: "As you complete this study of Declaration principles in thought and action, we hope you can give a heartfelt 'Amen' to these words." This is an appropriate response to a Christian sermon, but not to an objective history curriculum that is supposed to stimulate critical thinking, not unthinking acquiescence.

If a public school were to introduce such a religiously proselytizing curriculum, it would, in my view, be unconstitutional. Under the First Amendment religion may not be preached in the public schools in the guise of false history, any more than creationism can be smuggled into the public schools under the banner of false science.

In a recent case in Kearny, New Jersey, a public high school teacher of eleventh-grade students "told his sixth-period students at Kearny High School that evolution and the Big Bang were not scientific, that dinosaurs were aboard Noah's ark, and that only Christians had a place in heaven, according to audio recordings made by a student whose family is now considering a lawsuit claiming Mr. Paszkiewicz broke the church-state boundary."[19]

> According to a report in the *Observer*, a local New Jersey newspaper, Mr. Paszkiewicz was recorded saying of Jesus: "If you reject his gift of salvation, then you know where you belong. He did everything in his power, suffered your pains for you, and he's saying, 'Please, accept me, believe.' If you reject that, you belong in hell."[20]

The Williams Case: Was the Declaration Banned?

There is a prevalent urban (or perhaps rural) myth, propagated by the right-wing media, that a public school teacher was prevented from teaching the Declaration of Independence to fifth-grade students in a historically accurate way because it refers to the "Creator." Nothing can be farther from the truth. To begin with the incident around which the myth has grown, the Declaration was displayed on the walls of the school and featured in the fifth graders' textbooks. Even Stephen Williams, the teacher who sued his school board, acknowledged that it's "a little bit of a stretch" to say that "the Declaration was banned."[21] What Williams sought to offer the students was a highly edited version of the Declaration, focusing on references to God, along with portions of other historical documents carefully selected to present an orthodox Christian perspective.

Yet this is the way the dispute was characterized by the Religious Right and their media supporters. A lawyer for the Alliance Defense Fund, which sued the school district on behalf of the teacher, issued a press release blaring, "Declaration of Independence Banned from Classroom." It went on to excoriate the district for its alleged decision to "censor" "documents like the Declaration of Independence."[22] The *Drudge Report* picked up the false story and ran with it, screaming, "Declaration of Independence Banned at California School!"[23] On national TV, Newt Gingrich said that a "high school history teacher"—the controversy actually involved a fifth-grade teacher—"was not allowed to give out the Declaration of Independence because it has the words 'Our Creator' in it, and I think that is literally an attack on the very core concept of America."[24] MSNBC ran an item with the title "School Bans History Materials Referring to God; Calif. Teacher Prohibited from Giving Declaration of Independence."[25]

And the right-wing media and organizations ran with it as well. Sean Hannity told his audience, "Plus, could an American school ban the Declaration of Independence? You're not going to believe it. It actually happened." Later in the program, Alan Colmes echoed his cohost: "And later, one school has banned the use of historical documents such as the Declaration of Independence because of its reference to God."[26] John Gibson, who sat in for Bill O'Reilly and hosted *The O'Reilly Factor*, said that "the Declaration of Independence is banned from a California classroom—where else?—because it contains the word God."[27] George Landrith, president of the conservative organization Frontiers of Freedom, wrote, "The Declaration of Independence and the Boy Scouts are unconstitutional and pose a grave danger to America's freedoms—if you believe the left and the American Civil Liberties Union."[28]

I have read the handouts Mr. Williams sought to distribute to his fifth-grade students.[29] They constitute one of the most insidious efforts I have ever witnessed to brainwash eleven-year-old children into accepting Christianity, the divinity of Jesus, "intelligent design," and other beliefs central to the proselytizing agenda of the Religious Right. The technique he employs is particularly sneaky, especially when directed at preteenagers. He picks and chooses from historical documents and selectively distributes *only* those that promote Christianity. The children are not told, of course, that there are many other, equally historical and relevant materials that have been deliberately censored by Williams, and that they are being misled and miseducated by his highly biased selection and editing of sources. I am including extensive examples to give a representative illustration of Williams's tactic, but a complete reading of his handouts is necessary to get the full picture of his manipulation and deception.

Let us begin with Thomas Jefferson, whom he has the nerve to include in his listing of "What Great Leaders Have Said about the Bible." This is what Williams would have his eleven-year-old students believe are Thomas Jefferson's views on the Bible: "The Bible makes the best people in the world." This would suggest to impressionable students that Jefferson loved the Bible, believed that it was the word of God, and thought that it would be good for children to study it. As we have seen, this is precisely the opposite of what Jefferson actually said in his voluminous writings about the Bible. The students would not be told that Jefferson did not approve of the commandment visiting the sins of the father upon the children, that he believed that the story that the Ten Commandments came from God "is so defective and doubtful . . . that we have a right . . . to entertain much doubt what parts of them are genuine,"[30] and that he opposed the "reading of the Bible by schoolchildren" until they were about seventeen years old and could "[q]uestion with boldness even the existence of God."[31]

Williams would surely not tell his students that Jefferson reserved his greatest contempt for the New Testament, which he believed consisted of "so much absurdity, so much untruth, charlatanism and imposture"[32] that he characterized it as "dung"[33] and its authors as "ignorant, unlettered men" who borrowed the story of the Holy Trinity from Greek mythology.[34] Williams would not have his students read the following statement by Jefferson: "[T]he day will come when the mystical generation of Jesus by the Supreme Being as His Father, in the womb of a virgin, will be classed with the fable of the generation of Minerva in the brain of Jupiter."[35]

The students are then given the views of John Adams: "The Bible is the best book in the world. It contains more than all the libraries I have seen."[36] Williams purports to present students with "John Adams' Diary," but he rummages through thousands of entries, many of them skeptical with regard to Christianity, and selects only those entries that present an orthodox Christian perspective. He includes the following:

The great and Almighty author of nature, who at first established those rules which regulate the world, can as easily suspend those laws whenever his providence sees sufficient reason for such suspension. This can be no objection, then, to the miracles of Jesus Christ. Although some very thoughtful and contemplative men among the heathen attained a strong persuasion of the great principles of religion, yet the far greater number, having little time for speculation, gradually sunk into the grossest opinions and the grossest practices. These, therefore, could not be made to embrace the true religion till their attention was roused by some astonishing and miraculous appearances. Ill reasoning of philosophers, having nothing surprising in them, could not overcome the force of prejudice, custom, passion, and bigotry. But when wise and virtuous men commissioned from heaven, by miracles awakened men's attention to their reasonings, the force of truth made its way with ease to their minds.

Williams excludes the religiously dissident views of the second president, which led his biographer, David McCullough, to conclude that Adams was repelled by the spirit of dogmatism and bigotry that he observed in "clergy and laity" alike, and favored reason over blind faith.

What Williams did not tell his students was that John Adams was a unitarian who rejected the Trinity as "fictitious miracles," the "Holy Ghost, and the priesthood, in favor of the God of nature and human reason."[37]

The views of other "great leaders"—such as Thomas Paine, who wrote *Common Sense*, the most important book leading up to the Declaration of Independence—are not included in the handouts, because they would undercut the propaganda effort being made by Williams. Here is what Paine said about the Bible:

[I]t is the fable of Jesus Christ, as told in the New Testament, and the wild and visionary doctrine raised thereon, against which I contend. The story, taking it as it is told, is blasphemously obscene. . . . [The virgin birth story] is upon the face of it, the same kind of story of Jupiter and Leda and Jupiter and Europa or any of the amorous adventures of Jupiter; and shows . . . that the Christian faith is built upon the heathen mythology.[38]

And here is what he said about Christianity: "Of all the systems of religion that ever were invented, there is none more derogatory to the Almighty, more unedifying to man, more repugnant to reason, and more contradictory in itself, than this thing called Christianity." [39]

Included in the Williams handouts are numerous quotes from the New Testament, excerpts from William Penn's "Frame of Government of Pennsylvania," and the following (italics in original handout):

> This the Apostle teaches in divers of his epistles: "The law," says he, "was added because of transgressions." (Galatians 3:19) In another place, "Knowing that the law was not made for the righteous man; but for the disobedient and ungodly, for sinners, for unholy and profane, for murderers, for whoremongers, for them that defile themselves with mankind, and for manstealers, for liars, for perjured persons," (1 Timothy 1:8–10) etc.; but this is not all, he opens and carries the matter of government a little further: "Let every soul be subject to the higher powers; for there is no power but of *God*. The powers that be are ordained of *God*: whosoever therefore resisteth the power, resisteth the ordinance of *God*. For rulers are not a terror to good works, but to evil: wilt thou then not be afraid of the power? Do that which is good, and thou shalt have praise of the same." (Romans 13:1–3) "He is the minister of God to thee for good." (Romans 13:4) "Wherefore ye must needs be subject, not only for wrath, but for conscience' sake." (Romans 13:5) [40]

The handout is also replete with references to Jesus Christ, for example, in excerpts from George Washington's Prayer Journal. [41] The spellings are reproduced here as they appeared in the handout:

Almighty God, and most merciful father, who didst command the children of Israel to offer a daily sacrifice to thee, that thereby they might glorify and praise thee for thy protection both night and day, receive, O Lord, my morning sacrifice which I now offer up to thee; I yield thee humble and hearty thanks that thou has preserved me from the danger of the night past, and brought me to the light of day, and the comforts thereof, a day which is consecrated at thine own service and for thine own honor. Let my heart, therefore, Gracious God, be so affected with the glory and majesty of it, that I may not do mine own works, but wait on thee, and discharge those weighty duties thou requirest of me, and since thou art a God of pure eyes, and wilt be sanctified in all who draww near unto thee, who doest not regard the sacrifice of fools, nor hear sinners who tread in thy courts, pardon, I beseech thee, my sins, remove them from thy presence, as far as the east is from the west, and accept of me for the merits of thy son Jesus Christ, that when I come into thy temple, and compass thine altar, my prayers may come before thee as incense; and as thou wouldst hear me calling upon thee in my prayer, so give me grace to hear thee calling on me in thy word, that it may be wisdom, righteousness, reconciliation and peace to the saving of the soul in the day of the Lord Jesus. Grant that I may hear it with reverence, receive it with meekness, mingle it with faith, and that it may accomplish in me, Gracious God, the good work for which thou has sent it. Bless my family, kindred, friends and country, be our God & guide this day and for ever for his sake, who ay down in the Grave and arose again for us, Jesus Christ our Lord, Amen. [See the notes for more excerpts from the prayer.][42]

The Declaration curriculum omits what has been characterized as Washington's "famous gift of silence" with regard to religion. He sometimes recited the words of orthodox Christianity:

> [B]ut his behavior spoke. He would not kneel to pray, and when his pastor rebuked him for setting a bad example by leaving services before communion, Washington mended his ways in his austere manner: he stayed away from church on communion Sundays. He acknowledged Christianity's "benign influence" on society, but no ministers were present and no prayers were uttered as he died a Stoic's death.

The Declaration curriculum, in its handouts, also attacks "Papists," citing excerpts from Samuel Adams's *The Report of the Committee of Correspondence to the Boston Town Meeting*:

> In regard to religion, mutual toleration in the different professions thereof is what all good and candid minds in all ages have ever practiced, and, both by precept and example, inculcated on mankind. And it is now generally agreed among Christians that this spirit of toleration, in the fullest extent consistent with the being of civil society, is the chief characteristical mark of the Church. Insomuch that Mr. Locke has asserted and proved, beyond the possibility of contradiction on any solid ground, that such toleration ought to be extended to all whose doctrines are not subversive of society. The only sects which he thinks ought to be, and which by all wise laws are excluded from such toleration, are those who teach doctrines subversive of the civil government under which they live. The Roman Catholics or Papists are excluded by reason of such doctrines as these, that princes

excommunicated may be deposed, and those that they call heretics may be destroyed without mercy; besides their recognizing the Pope in so absolute a manner, in subversion of government, by introducing, as far as possible into the states under whose protection they enjoy life, liberty, and property, that solecism in politics imperium in imperio, leading directly to the worst anarchy and confusion, civil discord, war, and bloodshed.[43]

Support for the belief in "the miracles of Jesus Christ" is presented in a citation from founding father John Adams's diary:

The great and Almighty author of nature, who at first established those rules which regulate the world, can as easily suspend those laws whenever his providence sees sufficient reason for such suspension. This can be no objection, then, to the miracles of Jesus Christ. Although some very thoughtful and contemplative men among the heathen attained a strong persuasion of the great principles of religion, yet the far greater number, having little time for speculation, gradually sunk into the grossest opinions and the grossest practices. These, therefore, could not be made to embrace the true religion till their attention was roused by some astonishing and miraculous appearances. The reasoning of philosophers, having nothing surprising in them, could not overcome the force of prejudice, custom, passion, and bigotry. But when wise and virtuous men commissioned from heaven, by miracles awakened men's attention to their reasonings, the force of truth made its way with ease to their minds.[44]

The curriculum also documents in the handouts the superiority of Christianity by again citing John Adams's diary:

The Christian religion is above all the religions that ever prevailed or existed in ancient or modern times, the religion of wisdom, virtue, equity, and humanity, let the blackguard Paine say what he will; it is resignation to God, it is goodness itself to man. . . .

One great advantage of the Christian religion is that it brings the great principle of the law of nature and nations—Love your neighbor as yourself, and do to others as you would that others should do to you,—to the knowledge, belief, and veneration of the whole people. Children, servants, women, and men, are all professors in the science of public and private morality. No other institution for education, no kind of political discipline, could diffuse this kind of necessary information, so universally among all ranks and descriptions of citizens. The duties and rights of the man and the citizen are thus taught from early infancy to every creature. The sanctions of a future life are thus added to the observance of civil and political, as well as domestic and private duties. Prudence, justice, temperance, and fortitude, are thus taught to be the means and conditions of future as well as present happiness.[45]

And, in the last example of how the handouts interpret our history are quotations from colonial statutes that deny office-holding to any "person, who shall deny the being of God or the truth of the Protestant religion, or the divine authority either of the Old or New Testaments."[46] He does not, however, include the Constitution's command that "no religious Test shall ever be required as a Qualification to any Office or public Trust under the United States."[47]

In perhaps the most transparent effort to propagandize his fifth graders to his fundamentalist Christian beliefs, Williams sought to assign them an excerpt from an essay by Jean-Jacques Burlamaqui. Its connection to American history is tenuous at best. The essay is a full-blown theological defense of intelligent design and an attack on what would later become evolution. He presents the classic religious argument that "there is a design," a "visible reason in all works of nature," proof of "wisdom and understanding," and of "a Creator." He ridicules those "who have attributed all these phenomena to chance" as "so ridiculous a thought, that I question whether a more extravagant chimera ever entered into the mind of man."[48] What this sermon is doing in a curriculum on American history is unclear, but it surely deserves a place of honor in the catechisms of every fundamentalist Christian church and an important role in the Sunday school teachings of their ministers.

Williams should have been fired for incompetence as a history teacher, for his unfairness in the editing of source material, for providing fifth-grade students age-inappropriate readings, and for his unconstitutional effort to impose fundamentalist beliefs on his captive elementary school children who would have no ability to question his biased selection of sources. Instead, he was simply told by the school board to keep his lessons "objective, age appropriate, and in compliance with the curriculum prescribed by the District and not an attempt to influence a student's religious beliefs (or lack thereof)"[49]—in other words, what he should have been doing all along.

Yet Williams became the poster child for the Religious Right and their media choir who falsely cried "censorship" of the Declaration of Independence, while it was Williams who had censored and distorted the far more complex, diverse, and unorthodox views of the generation that produced the Declaration.

Imagine the outcry by the Falwells, the Hannitys, the

O'Reillys, and the Gingriches if a more secular fifth-grade teacher had tried to distribute heavily edited and ideologically selected source material that included only statements from the founding generation that rejected the Bible, denounced Christianity, and questioned the existence of God. As we have seen, there are many such statements, but no public school teacher would ever—or should ever—get away with suggesting to fifth graders that these statements are any more representative of the wide diversity of beliefs held by the founders than are the Christianocentric statements wrenched out of context and selectively served up by Williams.

The real complaint of the Religious Right in the Williams case was not over censorship or academic freedom; they would be the first to demand censorship of, and denial of academic freedom to, a teacher who was seeking to promote secularism, agnosticism, atheism, skepticism, or free thinking. Their complaint is that Christianity is not being promoted in the public schools.

Christianizing America

Lest anyone be fooled into believing that the ultimate goal of the Religious Right is merely to introduce some generic religion into the public square, rather than to convert America into a Christian theocracy, just listen to the words of their own leaders, especially those spoken to the "faithful" rather than to more general audiences. It quickly becomes clear that the campaign for nonsectarian references to God is merely a stalking horse for establishing Christianity—or Judeo-Christianity, as it is now sometimes referred to—as our national religion. Listen to Lou Sheldon, the founder of the Traditional Values Coalition: "We [Christians] *were here first.* . . . We are the keepers of what is right and what is wrong."

And listen to Ralph Reed, the director of the Christian Coalition: "What Christians have to do is to *take back* the country. . . . I honestly believe that in my lifetime we will see a country once again governed by Christians. . . . and Christian values."

And to Jerry Falwell: "I hope to see the day when as *in the early days of our country*, we won't have any public schools. The churches will have taken them over again and Christians will be running them. . . . We must never allow our children to forget that this is a Christian nation. *We must take back what is rightfully ours*." (Emphasis added throughout these paragraphs.)

And to Pat Robertson:

> The Constitution of the United States . . . is a marvelous document for self-government by Christian people. But the minute you turn the document into the hands of non-Christian people and atheist people, they can use it to destroy the very foundation of our society. And that's what's been happening. . . . If Christian people work together, they can succeed . . . in *winning back* control of the institutions that have been *taken from them over the past 70 years*.

Robertson goes on to claim that "our nation's spiritual *heritage* is being systematically eliminated from the *historical record*," and that the real Americans are being denied an honest look "at our nation's past." In a foul bit of immigrant-bashing, he opposes "anyone running the foreign affairs of America who speaks with a foreign accent" and asks, "How can anyone who spent most of his life in Germany or Poland fully understand the family life, the shared values, the history of free enterprise and free speech and the intense patriotism of [real Americans] born in Columbus, Ohio?"

And then there is Pat Buchanan, who no longer speaks of our Judeo-Christian heritage, but instead rails against the "across-the-board assault on our Anglo-American heritage" and campaigns with nativist slogans and symbols.

This kind of nativist rhetoric, which is being echoed by the current resurgence of xenophobia in Poland, Germany, and Russia, pits the "real" Americans, the "original" Americans, the "Christian" Americans against these newcomers who would "change" the old system.

Nor do the "originalists" try to disguise the identity of the newcomers who are endangering the original Christian character of America. Listen to Ralph Reed: "[It is] the Jewish element of the ACLU which is trying to drive Christianity out of the public place . . . because the ACLU is made up of a tremendous amount of Jewish attorneys." Jewish analogies, and comparisons with the Holocaust, are a particular favorite of Pat Robertson: "Just like what Nazi Germany did to the Jews, so liberal [does he mean Jewish?] America is now doing to the Evangelical Christians. It's no different . . . more terrible than anything suffered by any minority in our history." As Robertson made this point, footage of Nazi atrocities against Jews was shown on a video monitor behind him.

More Robertson:

[I]t is obviously one thing to insure that the horrors of the Holocaust are never repeated again. . . . However, it is quite another thing for a strident minority within a minority of only 5,000,000 [here there is no doubt that he is referring to Jews] to regard the expression of the deeply held beliefs of the majority as so repugnant that it undertakes the systematic vilification, weakening and ultimate suppression of the majority point of view.

Robertson also told Larry King that the "slaughter [of] a million and a half babies [by abortionists] rivals—it exceeds—the Holocaust of Adolf Hitler." Trying to silence his critics, Robertson repeatedly invokes the Holocaust by placing *himself* in the position of the Jewish victims of the Nazis. When he was attacked by an op-ed article in the *Miami Herald*, Robertson replied that the attack reminded him of his recent visit to Dachau. He accused his critics of reeking "with the stench of Fascism" and being "the spiritual heirs of Joseph Goebbels." Then he asked, "Do you also have a ghetto chosen to herd the pro-life Catholics and evangelicals into? Have you designed the appropriate yellow patch that Christians should wear?" He answered these questions by telling his followers that "the same thing is happening to Christians in America today."

Of course, Robertson is lying through his teeth: Christians are still dominant in every aspect of American life. Indeed, that is precisely the reason civil libertarians are concerned about government entanglement with Christianity in particular; there is no realistic danger of Islam, Buddhism, or Judaism becoming the Established Church in America. Nobody is claiming that America is a Buddhist nation!

Other fanatics of the Christian right talk about a "religious cleansing" in America akin to what is occurring in the Balkans and what took place during the Holocaust: "Just as ethnic cleansing attempts to rid certain ethnic groups and their influence from public life, so religious cleansing attempts to do the same with religious groups."

These analogies to men, women, and children who were physically slaughtered are incredibly insensitive, especially in a nation where Christianity is the dominant religion, where every president is Christian and proclaims his belief in God, and where the Constitution and the courts vigorously enforce the free exercise of religion. The Christian right's attempt to wrap itself in the currently voguish mantle of victimization is a transparent one. Even some conservative Christians are sick and tired of this constant complaining by the most powerful religious majority in this free country. As one critic aptly put it, "The Apostle Paul would never have done such a thing. When the whole early church was being fed to the lions, they weren't whining."[50]

In addition to the Christian right's claim that Christians (by which they mean evangelical Protestants who agree with their view of religion and politics) are the "original" and "native" Americans and that newcomers with different religious views are invaders out to destroy Christian values, they also seek to move American politics from the center to the extreme right by "[taking] back the country, one precinct at a time, one neighborhood at a time and one state at a time." They reject centrist coalition politics and eschew democracy itself as "the great love of the failures and cowards of life," and refuse to subject their version of the gospel to a majority vote. Unless a political system produces a "Christian politics," with exclusively "Christian values" and successful "Christian candidates," they maintain that it should be changed to assure that "Christians" are elected and "humanists" are "removed from office."

At a time when ethnic and religious warfare is bloodying much of the world, America should count the blessings of the religious pluralism that has made this country so great and so stable. The Christian right wants to end all of this and bring religious warfare to our shores. Listen to Randall Terry's prescription for religious bloodshed: "I want you just to let a wave of intolerance wash over you. Yes, hate is good . . . our goal is a Christian nation. We have a Biblical duty, we are called by

God, to conquer this country. We don't want equal time. We don't want pluralism." Even the somewhat more moderate Pat Robertson sounds like he is urging a latter-day Armageddon:

> If Christian people work together, they can succeed during this decade [the 1990s] in winning back control of the institutions that have been taken away from them over the past 70 years. Expect confrontations that will not only be unpleasant but at times *physically bloody*. . . . Institutions will be plunged into wrenching change. We will be living through one of the most tumultuous periods in human history. When it is over, . . . God's people will emerge victorious. But no victory ever comes without a battle.

Let there be no mistake about the ultimate goal of the Christian right: to turn the United States into a *theocracy*, ruled by Christian evangelicals. "We are talking about Christianizing America. We are talking about simply spreading the gospel in a political context," says Paul Weyrich, founder of the Free Congress Foundation. Pat Robertson is equally frank: "I believe that [Jesus] is Lord of the government, and the church, and business and education, and hopefully, one day, Lord of the press. I see Him involved in everything. . . . I want the church to move into the world."

As a first step on the road to fulfilling their theocratic program, the Christian right seeks to lower the wall of separation between church and state. Robertson calls separation of church and state "a lie of the left." Falwell calls it a "rape [of] the Constitution." And Reverend W. A. Criswell, the man who delivered the benediction at the 1984 Republican national convention, says there is "no such thing as separation of church and state"; it is "a figment of the imagination of infidels." Others regard it as "blasphemy" and a rejection of "God's law." Although the Christian Coalition now claims that there is "a lively debate" within its ranks over the separation of church and state, an analysis of statements made by its leaders to its members makes it clear that it is a one-sided debate.[51]

Rarely mentioned by these fundamentalists is the historical fact that Thomas Jefferson borrowed the phrase "separation of church and state" from Roger Williams, who coined it primarily as a means of protecting *churches* against state intervention. The legal historian Mark DeWolfe Howe summarized the history this way: "When the imagination of Roger Williams built the wall of separation, it was not because he was fearful that without such a barrier the arm of the church would extend its reach. It was, rather, the dread of the worldly corruptions which might consume the churches if sturdy fences against the wilderness were not maintained."[52] When Jefferson borrowed the term, he intended a broader scope that also included protecting the rights of religious dissidents, including those who believed in no god, as well as preventing any establishment of religion in order to separate government power from organized churches.

As Alexis de Tocqueville—who is selectively quoted in the Declaration curriculum—recognized when he wrote *Democracy in America* in 1835, "State religions [may] serve the interests of political power [but] they are always sooner or later fatal for the church." He further observed that "religion flourished here because it had been separated from government," in contrast to Europe, "with its history of religious warfare and dying churches." Currently, as well as historically, the separation of church and state benefits religion in America. A greater percentage of citizens attend church, believe in God, and proclaim that they are religious in this country than in any nation with an established church- or state-supported religious education: "National polls on religion report that 19 out of every 20 people affirm a faith in God, a majority say grace at mealtime and 2 out of every 5 say they regularly attend services in a church, synagogue or mosque."[53] Garry Wills has summarized the contemporary relationship as follows: "The first nation to disestablish religion remains a marvel of religiosity."[54]

But this is not enough for the Christian right. These politically ambitious preachers want the power of government at their disposal both to serve their right-wing political agenda and to help proselytize for their God. They regard the establishment of Christianity in America as a direct order from God. They want to declare the United States a "Christian nation," governed by the laws of Jesus: "a Bible-based social, political, and religious order," in which Jesus "is Lord of the government." Some members of the Christian right even reject the concept of "toleration" of other religious beliefs. They want a theocracy "which denies the religious liberty of the enemies of God."[55]

When speaking to each other, many of the Religious Right are quite candid about their goal of Christianizing America. A book by the authors of Christian best sellers, D. James Kennedy and Jerry Newcombe, is titled *What If America Were a Christian Nation Again?* In it they quote snippets from early Americans who did regard our nation as Christian, whatever that might mean in light of our Constitution's prohibition of religious tests or any establishment of religion. A justice of the Supreme Court did express his opinion in 1892 that we are a Christian nation.[56] He did so in the context of construing the language of an immigration law barring businesses from prepaying, contracting, or otherwise encouraging laborers to come to America for employment purposes. The Court found that the statute did not proscribe an English minister, solicited to preside over a church in New York City, from entering the country. The Court ruled that the law was meant only to burden the passage of unskilled wage laborers. Justice David J. Brewer, writing for the Court, reasoned as follows:

> These, and many other matters which might be noticed, add a volume of unofficial declarations to the mass of organic utterances that this is a Christian nation. In the face of all these, shall it be believed that a Congress of the United States intended to make it a misdemeanor for a church of this country to contract for the services of a Christian minister residing in another nation?[57]

The same justice expressed contempt, bordering on bigotry, against other religions when he favorably quoted Chancellor Kent of the Supreme Court of Judicature of New York for the proposition that the Court is not bound

> by any expressions in the Constitution as some have strangely supposed, either not to punish at all, or to punish indiscriminately, the like attacks upon the religion of Mahomet or of the Grand Lama; and for this plain reason, that the case assumes that we are a Christian people, and the morality of the country is deeply engrafted upon Christianity, and not upon the doctrines or worship of those impostors.[58]

In other words, the Constitution—according to the absurd reasoning of Chancellor Kent and Justice Brewer—would allow discrimination against Muslims and Buddhists, because they are religious "impostors," but not against Christians, because that is the true religion. That, of course, is precisely what Dennis Prager *is* proposing, though he would probably describe our true religion as "Judeo-Christian." This is a poor provenance on which on which to base a claim that we are, as a matter of constitutional law, a Christian nation.[59]

It is an argument, moreover, that goes too far. After he retired from the Supreme Court, David J. Brewer delivered lectures in which he claimed—quite falsely—that the Supreme Court had "formally declared" that ours is a "Christian nation." In support of this conclusion he cited numerous colonial and early American statutes that require a belief in Christianity as a condition to holding office or even of securing the protection of the law. But many of these statutes explicitly *omitted* Catholics. They required adherence to "the Protestant religion" (page 23), to "the true Christian faith now professed in the Church of England" (page 13), to "the pure gospel of Christ, our only Mediator" (an obvious reference to the Pope [page 21]). Many of the colonists and of the founding generation were virulently anti-Catholic. Yet few today would claim we are a Protestant nation, despite the anti-Catholic provenance of the cited sources.

Nor is the recent context in which this issue arose any more compelling, either morally or legally. In 1989, Justice Sandra Day O'Connor complied with a request from an archconservative Arizona Republican friend who had asked her to write a letter in support of a proposed Republican Party resolution declaring the United States to be "a Christian Nation . . . based on the absolute law of the Bible." Justice O'Connor's reply—written on Court stationery and later circulated as part of a successful campaign to have the Arizona Republican Party adopt the Christian Nation Resolution—included the following: "You wrote me recently to inquire about any holdings of this Court to the effect that this is a Christian Nation. There are statements to such effect in the following opinions: Church of the Holy Trinity v. United States. Zorach v. Clauson. McGowan v. Maryland."

In addition to the impropriety of a Justice lending the Court's judicial imprimatur to a controversial partisan proposal, Justice O'Connor's case citations were just plain wrong. The last two cases do not contain any statements of support for the claim that "this is a Christian Nation." Indeed, their entire thrust is to the contrary. The first opinion does—the one by Justice Brewer—but it also contains the discredited bigotry of the past age.

No Court decision over the last 114 years lends any support to the claim that we are a "Christian Nation." There are statements that we are a "religious people," but they are invariably followed by assurance of "no partiality to any one group."

When her letter was publicly disclosed, Justice O'Connor issued a statement through the Court press office regretting that the "letter she had written to an acquaintance . . . was used in a political debate." The press office assured us that she "had no idea" the letter would be used politically. But the original request made it unmistakably clear that she was being asked to write her letter specifically for use in the campaign for the Christian Nation Resolution being pressed by elements in the Republican Party. This is the relevant language in the request: "Republicans are making some interesting advances in this heavily controlled Democratic area. Some of us are proposing a resolution which acknowledges that the Supreme Court ruled in 1892 that this is a Christian Nation. It would be beneficial and interesting to have a letter from you." Not only was Justice O'Connor's letter used in that campaign, its miscitation of cases was relied on in the resolution enacted by the Arizona Republican Party. That resolution begins, "Whereas the Supreme Court of the United States has three holdings to the effect that this is a Christian nation," then cites the decisions provided by Justice O'Connor and declares that we are "a Christian Nation," and that the Constitution created "a republic based upon the absolute laws of the Bible, not a democracy." Justice O'Connor was widely rebuked for her unethical foray into Republican partisan and religious politics and her miscitation of history.

It is simply false, as a matter of history, to claim as some do:

> The records of each era of America's history have already declared this to be a Christian nation, and there still remain volumes of additional evidence. For example, the writings of prominent Founding Fathers add yet more to the volume of "organic utterances" already confirming the Court's 1892 declaration that "this is a Christian nation."[60]

But this false history is widely accepted by many on the Religious Right as a full and thoughtful account of the American experience.

The "battle" being waged by the Christian right is *not*, therefore, a minor dispute over whether there should be silent prayer in schools or merely a moment of silent contemplation, nor is it an argument over crèches and menorahs in the town square. These divisive issues are simply the tactical stalking horses for a much larger war plan to turn the United States into a Christian theocracy in which non-Christians are actively proselytized and, if they do not convert, are deemed *officially* and *legally* to be—at best—second-class citizens, as they have always been in countries where Christianity is the established state religion.

In addition to demanding prayer in the schools, an end to abortion, and the denial of equal rights to gays, the Christian right also espouses the traditional political, economic, and social agenda of the Republican right wing, including tax reduction, the end of welfare, the rollback of civil rights, and the instituting of "law and order." Indeed, the Christian right argues that there is no distinction between the *religion* of the right and the *politics* of the right, since there should be no separation between church and state. David Limbaugh, an advocate for the Religious Right, equates "value voters" with "Christian voters," as if non-Christians cannot support strong moral values. "Secular" has become a dirty word—even a code word for immoral. And humanist, as in "secular human-ist," is even worse.

As recently as August 2006, Katherine Harris, a Republican congresswoman from Florida who was running for the U.S. Senate, said the following: "If you are not electing Christians, tried and true, under public scrutiny and pressure, if you're not electing Christians then in essence you are going to legis-late sin."[61] Harris lost. She was not the first American to play the religious bigotry card in an election:

In 1996, independent and Republican voters in Kansas were urged to vote for Rep. Sam Brownback over his Democratic challenger, Jill Docking, through telephone "push polls" that helpfully reminded listeners that Dock-ing was Jewish. And cited that as a good reason to vote against her. Come November, Docking lost.

Brownback insisted he knew nothing about the calls. But Docking's campaign communications manager, Scott Swenson, says that Brownback's campaign and the Kansas Republican Party constantly referred to Docking as "'Jill Sadowsky Docking' in press releases and in rhetoric. Many reporters commented on how offensive they found it." Of course, that is her name, I say. "But what is the importance of it if not to put the name 'Sad-owsky' out there," says Swenson. "They were trying to call attention to the fact that Jill was Jewish." Docking agrees with this assessment.

Docking, reached in Wichita, Kansas, says such push polls are "a reality of life in America, and I don't think it will change." She also doesn't think the calls changed the outcome of the election. "Those people that would have substantially changed their vote because the push pollers told them I was Jewish probably wouldn't have voted for me anyway. If someone were not tolerant of Jews they were not my voter. But it was very uncomfortable and ugly."[62]

President George W. Bush not only ran as a Christian, he dedicated his first inaugural to—in the words of the evangelical minister who blessed the event—"*our* savior. [Emphasis added.]"[63] By choosing to invoke "the Father, the Son, the Lord Jesus Christ" in blessing the presidency during his inauguration, President Bush set the tone for the rest of his days in the White House, which have been marked by ongoing efforts to utilize his position to promote and perpetuate the idea of America as a Christian nation.

A prime example is a bill signed by President Bush in August 2006 designating the forty-three-foot-tall Christian cross located atop the Mt. Soledad military cemetery in La Jolla, California, as a federal war memorial, thus placing it under the control of the Department of Defense. The cross, which was erected in 1954, had been declared by a federal judge in May 2006 to be a violation of the separation of church and state. The judge ordered the cross removed from the municipally owned land on which it stood, but before the removal order was carried out, the Supreme Court ordered a stay to resolve pending legal issues. During this delay, congress passed a bill, signed into law by President Bush, making the Mt. Soledad cross, and the ground below it, federally controlled land. Supporters of the cross hoped that placing it under control of the federal government would increase the chances that the Supreme Court would reverse the lower court's decision and allow it to remain standing, since the U.S. Constitution "is more flexible about religious icons on federal property than the state Constitution is about city land."[64]

I recently visited this cross. It is quite beautiful and dramatic. If the land on which it is located were to be sold or given to private individuals or groups and it were no longer supported by the federal or state government, there would be no constitutional problem. But those who seek to Christianize America want the cross to be sponsored by government precisely to make an unconstitutional point!

An attempt to Christianize the American military is currently being made through a provision, buried deep within a Pentagon spending bill, that would allow military chaplains to "pray according to the dictates of their own conscience," even at mandatory events. If passed, the provision would effectively undermine a rule recently promulgated by the military that specifically *prohibits* chaplains from using sectarian language in prayers offered during mandatory military functions such as changes of command. This rule, announced in February 2006, was intended as a "response to a 2004 episode at the Air Force Academy in which cadets accused evangelical Christians in high-ranking positions of proselytizing and discrimination."[65] If congressional conservatives are successful in passing the spending bill with the provision intact, future Christian chaplains would have license to continue in the discriminatory footsteps of their forebears, who "in such cases have long invoked Christ."[66] In the conference committee, however, the language stated that "each chaplain shall have the prerogative to pray according to the dictates of the chaplain's own conscience, except as must be limited by military necessity, with any such limitation being imposed in the least restrictive manner feasible."[67]

In addition to protecting the "right" to promote Christianity on public land or during military ceremonies, the Bush administration has also created opportunities for U.S. foreign-aid dollars to be utilized by groups that engage in aggressive proselytization, thus creating the impression, if not the reality, that the federal government is sponsoring efforts to convert foreigners to Christianity.[68] While the U.S. policy in the past had been to give federal money only to religious organizations that maintained a clear wall of separation between their general aid efforts and proselytization, many of these rules have been either relaxed or completely removed under the direction of President Bush. Though some of these changes were accomplished through legislation, the president himself has been personally responsible for some, at times utilizing executive orders to push through his "faith-based initiatives" when Congress was unwilling to enact them into law.[69] Bush has openly taken credit for such policy changes, in one instance proudly telling a gathering of faith-based groups that "Congress wouldn't act, so I signed an executive order—that means I did it on my own."[70]

While the relaxed policies should theoretically benefit religious organizations of all denominations and faiths, a survey conducted by the *Boston Globe* showed that Christian groups received 98.3 percent of all federal foreign-aid funding from 2001 to 2005, which amounted to $1.7 billion.[71] Groups such as World Vision, which openly mix messages of health care and education with those about belief in Jesus and eternal salvation, have been the prime beneficiaries of the newly broadened rules for federal foreign aid, since the old policies prohibited U.S. funds from reaching organizations that made no attempt to separate explicitly religious activities from federally-sponsored aid programs.[72] The end result is that U.S. dollars are now being used to support groups whose members "preach about Jesus while teaching breast-feeding and nutrition," thus leaving the aid recipients with the impression that the United States government is supporting the efforts aimed at their proselytization and conversion to Christianity.

While the Religious Right is quick to claim that their crusade to convert the United States into a Christian nation would not mean second-class status for non-Christians, the actions of some of their most vocal activists reveal discrimination even against Mormons, who believe their religion to be part of Christianity.[73] Amy Sullivan, writing in *Washington Monthly*, reported, "In 2004, Mormons were specifically excluded from participation in the National Day of Prayer organized by Shirley Dobson (wife of James Dobson, leader of the conservative Christian organization Focus on the Family), because their theology was found to be incompatible with Christian beliefs."[74]

The *Economist* reported in September 2006, "Opinion polls suggest that anti-Mormon feeling is one of the most enduring religious prejudices in America. An *L.A. Times/Bloomberg* poll in June found that 37 percent of Americans would not vote for a Mormon presidential candidate; other polls put the figure at 17 percent."[75]

Some go so far as to claim that the separation of church and state is unconstitutional: "[t]he contemporary courts, in their strong war against Christianity, have been forceful and effective both in ignoring history and in promoting their view on the separation of church and state. Not only does the nation **not** realize that separation of church and state is **un**constitutional, many are not even aware that the privilege to exercise religious freedom is constitutional! . . . How did this nation's attitude toward Christianity and government get turned upside-down? How did we ever abandon our roots?" (Emphasis in original.)[76] George F. Will has made the following interesting observations:

> [w]hen the most reliable predictor of a voter's behavior is whether he or she regularly attends church services, it is highly unlikely that Republicans would nominate a Unitarian. In 1967, when Gov. George Romney of Michigan evinced interest in the Republican presidential nomination, his Mormonism was of little interest and hence was no impediment. Four decades later, the same may not be true if his son Mitt, also a Mormon, seeks the Republican nomination in 2008.[77]

Nor are those who claim that the Declaration of Independence baptized America as a Christian nation likely to change their parochial views by studying the actual history of the founding of our nation by patriots who were seeking to make a clean break with the clerical influences on European governments. Even the clearest statement of principle, included in a treaty initiated by our first president, George Washington, and completed by our second president, John Adams, will not persuade those who are determined to see a Christian America. But for those with any concern for historical accuracy, the plain words of the Treaty of 1797 with Tripoli should be dispositive as to the intentions of the founding generation. The treaty ratified by the Senate, and the law of the land, declared, "The government of the United States is not in any sense founded on the Christian religion."[78] "Not in any sense!"

As we have seen and shall see, the actual views of the founding generation with regard to God, organized religion, and the separation of church and state are far more complex, diverse, and interesting than caricatures drawn by the Religious Right.

3

What Are "the Laws of Nature and of Nature's God"?

Why "Natural Law" Was Invoked

The Religious Right, in its effort to Christianize America, points to the fact that according to the Declaration of Independence, the right of the colonists to separate from Great Britain was based on "the Laws of Nature and of Nature's God." This resort to "natural law" raises profound questions as to the source, basis, and "unalienab[ility]" of this or any other "right." "Natural" law, as distinguished from "positive" legal enactments, is not necessarily found in any codified legislation or judicial decisions. It derives from divine or natural principles rather than from "the consent of the governed." When a right does emanate from "the consent of the governed"—from existing positive legal enactments such as the Constitution or the Bill of Rights—its source is more readily identifiable and its significance more easily understood. We find comfortable justification for the moral force of this consent in the basic tenets of democratic theory, social contract, and other currently accepted values. The people themselves, the "governed," have decided to entrench, in our governing documents, certain fundamental liberties and limitations, which they designate as "rights," rather than mere preferences, and make these rights difficult to repeal, even by subsequent majorities.

Our own Constitution requires a deliberately cumbersome amending process. Though it has been invoked numerous times throughout our history, it has generally been used to expand rights (such as the right to vote), to create new rights (such as the right not to be enslaved and to equal protection of the laws), and to correct errors or anachronisms in the original document that became evident on the basis of new experiences (such as the development of the party system). No fundamental right, once created by the positive law of our Constitution, has ever been repealed. In fact, it is fair to say that most of the rights enumerated in the original Constitution and Bill of Rights have been expanded by judicial construction (a uniquely American genre of positive law) beyond their original intent.

This does not necessarily mean that such positive rights are "unalienable"—either in practice or in theory. For example, during wars and other national emergencies, many rights deemed fundamental during peacetime have been restricted, at least temporarily. Even now, following the events of September 11, 2001, we are seeing certain rights contracting before our very eyes—or even worse, deliberately hidden from our view by claims of necessary secrecy. Since the current national security emergency is not likely to end in the foreseeable future, these contractions may be long-term if not permanent. The rights that have been curtailed may not be among the most fundamental—at least for those not directly affected—but certainly they are not trivial.

The point is that rights lie along a continuum of importance, and the more fundamental they are, the more likely they are to be seen as "unalienable." Rights also lie along a continuum of generality, with "Life, Liberty, and the Pursuit of Happiness" at the most general and abstract end, and more "technical" rights, such as those announced in the *Miranda* decision, at the most specific and concrete end. The more abstract a right, the more "unalienable" (and uncontroversial) it will seem, since rights articulated at a high level of abstraction can mean all things to all people and can change in content over time and place without alienating the broad terms of the right itself.

The abstract rights articulated in the Declaration were not derived from positive—that is, enacted—law. These included the right to secede and the rights to life, liberty, and the pursuit of happiness. It would be interesting to speculate about which other rights might have been in the minds of the drafters. Perhaps the Bill of Rights, adopted ten years later, provides some clues. The rights enumerated in the Declaration, however, did not rely on any governing legislation or judicial decision. The Declaration did not invoke the "known law and statutes" of Great Britain, as the English Declaration of Rights had done in 1689. That should not be surprising, since the primary purpose of the Declaration was to provide a justification for an extralegal action—the "treasonous" and "criminal" act of secession and separation. Indeed, had the revolution failed, its leaders would certainly have been subject to criminal prosecution. In the absence of binding international law that provided for the right of secession or self-determination, there was no positive law to which the colonists could appeal for justification of their actions.

The classic alternative to positive law has, since the time of the Greeks and then Aquinas, been "natural law." Another alternative has been "the law of necessity" (thought to be an oxymoron by some), which finds some support both in natural and positive law. The Declaration, in fact, invoked such necessity in its formulation as well. "Natural law" based on divine revelation—the source of Christian natural law for Aquinas—was anathema to Jefferson. Since there was no existing positive law that supported secession, and since Jefferson would not invoke revealed biblical law, he needed a source beyond positive law but within the realm of human reason and experience. Hence "the Laws of Nature and of Nature's God," which Jefferson and his fellow deists believed could be derived from observing the design of the universe and of human nature, as the Stoics had done centuries earlier. The right to secede, along with the rights to life, liberty, and the pursuit of happiness were, according to Jefferson, divinely revealed law, but in a very different sense than the laws of the Bible. They were, instead, revealed in the "Laws of Nature" and endowed to all human beings by "Nature's God." Moreover, it did not take a philosopher, a prophet, or a theologian to translate these laws to the average person. They were "self-evident" in the sense that they were "impressed on the sense of every man"[1] who was equipped with an innate moral sense of right and wrong. Jefferson even thought that this moral sense was a *more* reliable way of discovering our rights than relying on abstract reason. He famously wrote, "State a moral case to a ploughman and a professor. The former will decide it as well, and often better than the latter, because he has not been led astray by artificial rules."[2]

It was thus unimportant to Jefferson whether the American colonists could offer abstract philosophical justifications for the natural rights that led them to demand their independence, because these farmers and merchants "felt their rights before they had thought of their explanation."[3] These rights were "law in the nature of man."[4] God had endowed human beings with their nature—which included a moral instinct—and this nature led inexorably to natural rights. According to Jefferson, man's instinctive moral sense is "as much a part of our constitution as that of feeling, seeing or hearing."[5] There is, as we shall see, a twofold problem with this approach to the source of rights—one logical, the other empirical. First, any approach that derives the "ought" of morality from the "is" of nature—even human nature—commits the classic "naturalistic fallacy." Second, even if moral conclusions could be drawn from nature, there is considerable doubt whether human beings are in fact born with an instinct for justice. Jefferson's observations about human nature, it turns out, may simply be untrue.

Does It Matter Whether "the Laws of Nature and of Nature's God" Exist?

In his seminal 1922 book *The Declaration of Independence*, Carl Becker argues that "to ask whether the natural rights philosophy of the Declaration of Independence is true or false is essentially a meaningless question."[6] He is wrong. The question of whether rights actually come from nature is meaningful and important. It is and always was an empirical question, subject to proof or disproof. It contains a null hypothesis. It is either true or false as a matter of fact, and it appears to be false by Jefferson's own standards of science and reason.

In the years since Jefferson—and Carl Becker—wrote, scientists have conducted experiments designed to determine whether human beings are born with certain dispositions, instincts, or attitudes. It would be impossible, of course, to establish, as a scientific matter, whether any such "inherent" characteristics, if they were indeed "impressed on the sense of every man," come from "their Creator," in the sense of an external God, or from some other, more biological, source. But it is possible, though quite difficult, to test for whether certain characteristics are more "inborn" or "acquired"—more "nature" or "nurture." This quest has been complicated by scientific findings that the structure of the brain, particularly the connections of synapses, continues to take shape not only in utero but even after birth. Thus nature is influenced by nurture even in something so basic as the physiology of the brain. These findings suggest that nature and nurture are on a continuum rather than separated by a sharp distinction, but they do not remove the question from the realm of scientific inquiry. If anything, these findings make this question even more subject to the complexities and nuances of science.[7]

Nor is there anything approaching consensus about the existence of a moral sense in the nonscientific literature. Some modern thinkers, such as the philosopher John Rawls, seem to believe that there is some "intuitionistic" predisposition toward justice. Rawls writes about "innate categories of morality common to all men imprinted in their neural structure."[8] Others, such as the legal philosopher Ronald Dworkin, reject that notion, pointing out that even in the United States and Britain, the majority of citizens "do not exercise the political liberties that they have, and would not count the loss of these liberties as especially grievous."[9] Such speculations, however, can hardly count as empirical, and the obvious disagreements among thinkers show that the theory of an inborn moral sense is anything but self-evident.

The bottom line is thus that Jefferson's "observations" on human nature turn out to be empirically questionable at best. No valid scientific study has ever convincingly demonstrated a "gene" for justice, an instinct for liberty, or even an inborn predisposition toward the rights of others. The various rights he mentioned in the Declaration—secession, life, liberty, and the pursuit of happiness—do not seem to be "impressed on the sense of every man." They must be learned, and many human beings around the world seem to have difficulty learning them. Far too many place little value on the lives of others; they welcome authority; and they accept lives of misery. Dostoyevsky may have been closer to the truth when he observed, through one of his characters, that human beings crave "miracle, mystery, and authority"[10] and that "nothing has been more insupportable for a man and a human society than freedom."[11] On the basis of Dostoyevsky's view of what is impressed on the human mind, he predicted that if people begin "to build their tower of Babel without [the authority of the church], they will end, of course, with cannibalism."[12] This pessimistic assessment, too, may be off the mark, but it is an empirical assessment, subject to the canons of science and the null hypothesis, just as Jefferson's more optimistic assessment of human nature is capable of being proved right or wrong. And it matters greatly whether it is Jefferson or Dostoyevsky who is closer to the truth. It is anything but "essentially meaningless" to ask whether "the natural rights philosophy of the Declaration of Independence is true or false," as Becker argued, since an empirically based philosophy cannot serve as a foundation for human rights if its essential underlying factual assumptions are false.

One reason why it is important—and certainly not "essentially meaningless"—to question the empirical basis of Jefferson's natural law is that if Jefferson were correct about rights being "impressed on the sense of every man," then the need for *legally entrenched rights* would actually *diminish*. It is precisely because most people have little appreciation for rights—at least until they or their loved ones stand to benefit from them in the short term—that it is so important to build them into the structure of government, as the United States subsequently did in the Constitution and the Bill of Rights. Rights, to the extent that they are different from the mere preferences of shifting majorities, are what Ronald Dworkin calls "trumps" on legislation, referenda, and other mechanisms of majority rule. Rights rule over preferences, even strong preferences. To designate something "a right" is to give it a special status above other interests. If all people—or even a constant majority of all people—had rights permanently "impressed" on their senses, there would be less need for such countermajoritarian (and in that sense undemocratic) trumps.

The rights enumerated by Jefferson in the Declaration were majoritarian in nature—at least in the context of separation from Great Britain. A majority of "one people" (colonial Americans) were being denied these rights by "another" people (Great Britain) and their king. They were *our* rights in relation to *them.* Perhaps self-serving rights are impressed on most human beings (along with self-serving nonrights), but the rights of *others,* which may take something away from *us,* must be learned from experience to be appreciated. A longer view is necessary to understand that granting rights to others—even when they disadvantage you in the short run—may be important to the stability of a society, and thus to the benefit of all in the long run. But most human beings seem to prefer the short-term certainty of immediate gratification to the long-term probability of more ultimate satisfaction. Rights, to the extent that they exchange immediate personal gratification for more long-term social stability, seem counterinstinctive.[13]

It should not be surprising that there was little controversy within the United States about the right to secede—that decision had already been made by the time the Declaration was ratified. The time for debate was over. This is not to suggest that the decision to secede itself was without controversy—there were many dissenters who remained to be persuaded—but even some who believed it would be imprudent to secede still believed there was a *right* to do so. There was even less controversy about the rights to life, liberty, and the pursuit of happiness, since those rights, stated abstractly, benefit everyone. The real rights controversy centered around the right of equality—if, indeed, the Declaration's expression of the "self-evident" truth "that all Men are created equal" was an assertion of a right at all. Any claim of equality benefits the less advantaged at the expense of the more advantaged. In the context of slavery, equality would come to mean—at least for abolitionists—that slaveowners could lose their valuable "property" if slaves were deemed their equals and thus not subject to their legal domination. As the Jefferson scholar Joseph J. Ellis has observed, "In 1861, for example, Lincoln thought the words of the Declaration justified a war against slavery, while leaders of the Confederacy thought the same words justified rebellion against the tyranny of the federal government led by Lincoln."[14]

The rights stated in the Declaration, however, are so abstract as to be nearly meaningless. If Jefferson could indeed assert them as self-evident, it was only because they are stated in so broad a manner that their controversial application to any particular problem of policy is obscured by the fog of generality. Everyone can agree on the importance of rights to life, liberty, and the pursuit of happiness, but only because agreement about such sweeping terms amounts to almost no binding agreement at all.

For example, the abstract right to life is uncontroversial, but when reduced to its particulars, it provokes the most divisive disputes. This right has been cited by opponents of abortion, capital punishment, assisted suicide, war, deadly force, animal rights, and other hot-button issues. It also has been cited by proponents of abortion (the mother's right to life), capital punishment (the rights of future victims), gun control, just war, deadly force, and medical research on animals. The right to life has become an emotional cliché equally available to all sides on every life-and-death issue.

The right to liberty has been invoked as the equivalent of John Stuart Mill's famous principle—articulated years after the Declaration—denying government the power to compel any individual to do, or refrain from doing, anything that has an impact only on the individual and not on other people. Jefferson anticipated Mill with regard to religious rights. His *An Act for Establishing Religious Freedom*—one of the three contributions for which he wanted to be remembered—included the following:

> that the opinions of men are not the object of civil government, nor under its jurisdiction; that to suffer the civil magistrate to intrude his powers into the field of opinion and to restrain the profession or propagation of principles on supposition of their ill tendency is a dangerous fallacy, which at once destroys all religious liberty, because he being of course judge of that tendency will make his opinions the rule of judgment, and approve or condemn the sentiments of others only as they shall square with or differ from his own; that it is time enough for the rightful purposes of civil government for its officers to interfere when principles break out into overt acts against peace and good order.[15]

The broad right to liberty can, of course, be invoked to justify any action. The British philosopher Jeremy Bentham believed that any law—even one prohibiting murder—is an "infraction" of liberty, but that many such infractions are justified by the greater good. So defined, the general right to liberty, as distinguished from more particular rights to specific liberties, becomes meaningless. Ronald Dworkin, in *Taking Rights Seriously,* has asked and sought to answer the question "Do we have a right to liberty?"

> Thomas Jefferson thought so, and since his day the right to liberty has received more play than the competing rights he mentioned to life and the pursuit of happiness. Liberty gave its name to the most influential political movement of the last century, and many of those who now despise liberals do so on the ground that they are not sufficiently libertarian. Of course, almost everyone concedes that the right to liberty is not the only political right, and that therefore claims to freedom must be limited, for example, by restraints that protect the security or property of others. Nevertheless the consensus in favor of some right to liberty is a vast one, though it is . . . misguided.[16]

Dworkin argues that belief in a right to liberty is misguided because equality is a more fundamental right and "laws are needed to protect equality, and laws are inevitably compromises of liberty."[17] Thus for Dworkin "in any strong sense of right, which would be competitive with the right of equality, there exists no general right to liberty at all."[18]

Other thinkers recognize additional claims against liberty, such as security, community, and responsibility. Under this view, liberty is what is left to the individual after other stronger or more legitimate claims have been satisfied, or at least balanced. If "Nature's God" is the God of the gaps, then liberty is the philosophy of the gaps.

The pursuit of happiness, like the right to liberty, is far too individualistic and open-ended to provide a blueprint, or even a general guide, for resolution of conflicting claims. What makes one person happy may make another miserable. H. L. Mencken once defined Puritanism as "the haunting fear that someone, somewhere may be happy." And George Bernard Shaw quipped: "Do not do unto others as they should do unto you—their tastes may be different." A general right to pursue happiness, like a general right to liberty, makes no specific policy claims—rather, it is what is left after other, competing, legitimate claims have been satisfied or balanced.

To characterize the right to secession or rights to life, liberty, and the pursuit of happiness as natural, God-given, and unalienable is to attribute to Nature and to God a prudential limitation on governmental power based on long and unhappy experiences with governments of unlimited powers—governments that also claimed to be based on the natural and divine "right" of rulers. But to make these rights seem natural or "self-evident" to people of varying natures, they must be stated in terms so abstract as to hide their sometimes controversial applications and to make them little more than clichés of comfortable consensus. As we will see, the authority to give them any *real* meaning lies with people, not with Nature or God.

Does Natural Law Exist, or Is It a Fiction?

Invoking natural law may be a useful, even sometimes effective, way of trumping other people's preferences in the absence of positive-law trumps, such as a constitution. For example, based on our current interpretation of the U.S. Constitution, a fetus has no constitutional right—or other positive-law right—not to be aborted if the mother so chooses. So antiabortion advocates invoke a natural-law "right to life" on behalf of the fetus. Some ground this natural-law right in their interpretation of divine revelation, while others ground it in their interpretation of the laws of nature. The same is true of the death penalty, which is explicitly authorized by the Constitution. Hence some opponents of capital punishment invoke the "right to life" even on behalf of convicted murderers.

Natural law, to those who believe in it, is an argument stopper—the ace of trumps. After all, if God Himself revealed the law, how can a mere mortal argue with it? Or if the law derives inexorably from Nature, how can it be wrong? As Juvenal put it: "Never does Nature say one thing and wisdom another."

Jeremy Bentham once quipped that people invoke natural law "when they wish to get their way without having to argue for it." To that I would add, "and without having to persuade a majority, or a court, to agree with them." It is right (and its opposite is wrong) just because they claim God or Nature said so. End of discussion. Bentham railed against the use of natural law in the Declaration of Independence, comparing it to witchcraft. He regarded natural law as "nonsense on stilts."

The most compelling argument for invoking natural law is that we need it. Without it we have no basis—at least no legal basis—for opposing or resisting unjust laws that have been properly enacted. British control of the colonies was legitimated by repeated acts of Parliament. It was lawful, at least according to English positive law. But Jefferson believed there were higher laws—"the Laws of Nature and of Nature's God"—that trumped English positive law, especially since the colonists were not represented in the English Parliament (as many, probably most, British subjects were not represented in those days of limited suffrage). It is not surprising that only a decade after the Declaration invoked natural law, the Constitution seemed to eschew reliance on anything but positive law—revolutionaries need natural law to justify their extralegal actions against the positive law of their enemies, but as soon as these same revolutionaries establish a new government, they can rely on "their own" positive law.

It is one thing to say that natural law is a useful, even essential, legal fiction for a civilized world. It is quite another thing to say that it actually exists. A cure for breast cancer would be useful as well, but until and unless one actually exists, it is fraudulent and dangerous to pretend that we have it. The reality is that natural law simply does not exist, no matter how much we "need" it or wish it existed. It is a human invention, much like organized religion. And it may be beneficial or harmful, much like organized religion. But even if it is beneficial, that doesn't make it any more real than a placebo that works.

There are, after all, only three basic sources of human knowledge: discovery, invention, and divine revelation. The physical rules of nature actually exist, and await discovery by human beings. (They would, of course, exist even in the absence of human beings, as they did for billions of years. They just would not be called "rules," because there would be no one to understand or even name them.) Newton discovered some, Einstein others, and Darwin yet others. If these giants had not discovered these rules when they did, it is reasonable to assume that other geniuses, who came after them, would have made these (or similar) discoveries, since the rules are out there waiting to be discovered, much as America was out there waiting to be found by Leif Eriksson or Christopher Columbus—or some other European, Asian, or African explorer—had the earlier explorers been drowned while attempting to cross the Atlantic. (America, like the rules of Nature, was also out there before human beings, and would

have remained there had it not been "discovered"—along
with its native population—by Europeans.)

Inventions are different. They require the creative com-
bining of different kinds of knowledge and information—both
theoretical and practical—to design something that did not
previously exist. Simple inventions, such as the cotton gin or
the automobile, would have been made by others if those
responsible for inventing them had never lived. Complex,
more individualistic inventions, such as Beethoven's sym-
phonies, Picasso's paintings, Shakespeare's plays, or Rube
Goldberg's contraptions, would never have been replicated by
others, at least not exactly. They are truly unique. We call
them "inspired," but they are human inventions. There are
also, of course, many things that fall somewhere between discovery and invention, and there are overlaps. This is because
inventions often require discoveries, and vice versa.

Finally, there is divine revelation, for those who believe in
it. Like discovery and invention, revelation lies along a continuum. Some people believe that God actually spoke to particular human beings, handed them tablets, or dictated entire
books. Others believe that God inspires human conduct in
ways that are not subject to human understanding. Yet others,
such as Jefferson and his fellow deists, believed that God created the rules of both physical and human nature, and that
any human being, by observing these rules, can see God's will
revealed (discovered) without the intermediation of churches,
Bibles, or ministers.

Into which of these categories do laws, rights, and morality
fit? Positive law is plainly a human invention. Madison's Constitution, for example, with its emphasis on division of power,
checks and balances, and separation of church and state, is an
experiment based on human experience—mostly negative—
with other types of government. Churchill seemed to agree

with this experimental approach when he characterized democracy as "the worst form of government except all those other forms that have been tried from time to time." It is an attempt to improve on the past (and on human nature). Like most human inventions, it builds on the prior inventions and discoveries of predecessors. Also like most inventions, it is imperfect and requires a process for its own change and improvement.

Natural law, on the other hand, purports to be a product of discovery and/or divine revelation. It is a fully developed and flawless entity, simply waiting to be discovered or discerned by human beings so they can live by its principles. As Jeremy Bentham once observed in a related context, this is "nonsense on stilts." It is supernatural superstition. There is simply no such thing waiting to be discovered, certainly nothing perfect and unchanging. All laws, in the sense of prescriptive rules of conduct and morality, are imperfect and ever-changing human inventions, for which we, as their inventors, are ultimately responsible. Natural law, and all of its variations, are also human inventions dressed up by humans as discoveries and divine revelations, to give them greater authority. They are, ultimately, no more than legal or moral fictions.

Is Natural Law a Necessary, or Even Useful, Fiction?

In addition to the question of whether natural law is a fiction—a human invention—there is the question of whether natural law is a beneficial or a harmful fiction. When it is invoked to produce a "good" result—to persuade individuals not to obey the "lawful" commands of evil tyrants—we all approve of it (ironically because we conclude that the end justifies the means—a very non-natural-law criterion for evaluating anything!). But we must recall that natural law also has been invoked in support of the worst of actions—including slavery, racism, sexism, and even terrorism.

At bottom, natural law is an invitation to self-righteous lawlessness (both positive and negative), in the sense that it provides a justification for refusing to obey positive law. We applaud such lawlessness when it is directed against Nazism and slavery, but often condemn it when it leads to terrorism, the blocking of abortion clinics, or the refusal to pay taxes. Natural law is a double-edged sword aimed at the heart of democracy and the rule of law, since these important mechanisms necessarily rely on a positive law equally accessible to all.

Jefferson himself used natural law and "natural rights" as an undemocratic tactic to discourage subsequent majorities from changing the good laws he wrote. In his *An Act for Establishing Religious Freedom*, Jefferson included a section containing the following admonition to future legislators:

> though we well know this Assembly elected by the people for the ordinary purposes of legislation only, have no power to restrain the acts of succeeding assemblies, constituted with the powers equal to our own, and that therefore to declare this act irrevocable would be of no effect in law; yet we are free to declare, and do declare, that the rights hereby asserted are of the natural rights of mankind, and that if any act shall be hereafter passed to repeal the present or to narrow its operation, such act will be an infringement of natural right.[19]

Thus, instead of trying to persuade the governed to make it difficult, by positive law, to amend the right to religious liberty, Jefferson played his trump card: natural law.

Jefferson believed it was a natural right of humankind not to be compelled "to furnish contributions of money for the propagation of opinions which he disbelieves"[20] and to "be free to profess, and by argument to maintain, their opinion in matters of religion."[21] I certainly agree that such rights *should* be recognized—indeed, entrenched—by the law, since experience demonstrates that if they are not recognized, many evils will follow. But I do not see them in nature. Even if the opposite were "natural"—even if there were a genetic predisposition toward believing in and imposing one true religion—I would still argue for the right to religious freedom and dissent. Nor does "revealed law" support these rights. Jefferson argued that if God, who is all-powerful, wanted everyone to follow the same religion, they would. This reductionist argument would also lead to the conclusion that if God wanted a world without murder, rape, and child abuse, we would be living in that world. The fact is that many religions—Catholicism, Puritanism, and Islam among them—have long advocated mandatory contributions to propagate their faith and punishment for those who advocate a different one. (While I was working on an earlier draft of this material, I read in the newspaper that the Catholic Church finally decided that it had been theologically improper to try to convert the Jews. Whoops! Sorry for all those inquisitions, crusades, and autos-da-fé. Previous popes were wrong—infallible, perhaps, but wrong.[22])

Jefferson's rights are important, not because human nature supports them, but because it does *not*. The right to dissent from the consensus of religious or other views reflects unnatural law—*nurtural* law—at its best. It is the function of rights to change human nature, or at least to provide a counterpoint to human nature, based on human experience.

A striking example of how natural law can be, and was,

used to produce evil results can be seen in an 1872 decision of the U.S. Supreme Court, denying women the right to practice law. In *Bradwell v. State of Illinois,* the lower court had invoked Jefferson's concepts of "natural law" and God as "designer" to argue that "God designed the sexes to occupy different spheres of action. It belonged to men to apply and execute the law."[23] The role assigned by nature to women was in the "domestic sphere." A justice of the Supreme Court invoked divine law: "The paramount destiny and mission of woman are to fulfill the noble and benign office of wife and mother. This is the law of the Creator."[24] We now recognize how downright stupid, ignoble, and malignant this divine design argument is, as applied to women by men, but even if it were somehow true that most women were "designed" by nature or told by God to stay home and darn the socks, it still would be wrong to deny a woman who wanted to challenge nature the right to try something she was not "designed" to do.

Natural law was used to justify slavery because of the "natural" differences between whites and blacks, and to support the criminalization of "unnatural" male homosexuality (which was called "the crime against nature"). What I have argued elsewhere about divine law also can be said about natural law:

> To be an advocate of divine law is to always have to say you're sorry for the mistakes of your predecessors, as your successors will inevitably have to apologize for the mistakes you are now making when you claim to know God's true intentions. It insults God to believe that it was he who mandated eternal inequality for women, execution for gays, slavery, animal sacrifice, and the scores of other immoral laws of the Bible, the Koran, and other

books that purport to speak in God's name. Humans are to blame for these immoralities, just as humans must be credited with the hundreds of morally elevating laws of these holy books. And it is humans who must continue to change law and morality so as to remain more elevated than the animals who indeed cannot rise above the law of nature and of the jungle. In a diverse world where many claim to know God's will, and where there is consensus about neither its content nor the methodology for discerning it, God should not be invoked as the source of our political rights. In any event, for the millions of good and moral people who do not believe in God, or in an intervening God—or who are agnostic about these matters—there must be other sources of morality, law, and rights.[25]

The fundamental flaw in any attempt to derive moral conclusions from the operation of nature is the failure to recognize that nature is morally neutral. As Robert B. Ingersoll correctly observed: "In nature there are neither rewards, nor punishments; there are only consequences." Its rules existed before human consciousness, and they would have operated even if no human being ever appeared in the world. Nature does what it does because of factors entirely irrelevant to human morality. As Anatole France once put it: "Nature has no principles, she furnishes us with no reason to believe that human life is to be respected. Nature, in its indifference, makes no distinction between good and evil." Anyone who seeks to derive moral conclusions directly from descriptions of nature necessarily indulges in a variation on what has been called the "naturalistic fallacy." This classic fallacy has been described in the following terms: "The naturalistic fallacy states that it is logically impossible for any set of statements of the kind usually called descriptive to entail a statement of the kind usually called evaluative." [26]

This is not to deny that there may be a relationship between nature and morality. Any attempt to build a system of morality that completely ignores nature will fail. Nature has a vote but not a veto on questions of morality. In deciding on a sexual morality appropriate for a given society, it is important to understand the nature of the sex drive. For example, efforts to deter adolescent masturbation as "unnatural" and therefore "wrong" are doomed to failure because the nature of adolescent sexuality is more powerful than the threats of punishment for this entirely harmless—and I would add "natural"—outlet. Many Catholics are now questioning whether priestly celibacy is incompatible with the natural sex drive. But even if sociobiologists were to prove that men are naturally inclined to force women into sexual submission, it would be morally wrong for a society not to make every reasonable effort to hold this "natural impulse" in check, because even if it is natural, it is wrong. "Doing what comes naturally" may be a good song title, but it is a terrible rule of morality. Rape is horribly wrong even though the men who wrote the Bible did not think it was wrong enough to include in the Ten Commandments while including voluntary adultery, but only if it involved a married *woman*! We can do better than the Ten Commandments because we have much more human experience on which to base our rules than did those very human beings who wrote the Bible.

Morality evolves with experience, and nature is part of that experience but not the only part. In constructing a moral code, one should not ignore the varieties of human nature, but the diverse components of nature cannot be translated directly into morality. The complex relationship between the *is* of nature and the *ought* of morality must be mediated by human experience. To ignore the complex relationships among nature, nurture, experience, and morality and to seek to derive moral conclusions directly from nature is to commit a particularly dangerous variation on the naturalistic fallacy. Patrick Buchanan misused nature when he characterized AIDS as "nature's retribution" against gay men for "violating the laws of nature,"[27] as did the ultra-Orthodox rabbi who declared the Holocaust to be God's punishment of the Jews for eating pork.

Among the most vocal indulgers in the naturalistic fallacy is Alan Keyes—former presidential candidate, national television talk show host, and prominent speaker. In a speech to impressionable public high school students at Hylton High School in Virginia, Keyes claims that to accept the scientific evidence in support of evolution—which he rejects because he does not believe that his "early relatives were monkeys"[28]—necessarily requires belief in the immoral principle that "might makes right" and that "justice" should come "only for the strong."[29] (This misguided claim is very different from arguing that belief in evolution will *lead* to belief in might makes right, which is an empirical claim that can be tested by science. Indeed, history seems to show that religious claims, which tend to be absolute, have been decided by might more often than by right.) He even erroneously claims that "this is what our children learn" in the public schools.[30] I would challenge him to cite a single example of this. He also suggests that this philosophy is what leads women to choose abortion, since the mother is stronger than the fetus. He argues, therefore, that we should not "respect" or "care about" the "results" of evolution.

This kind of confused thinking, which fails to understand the basic differences between the *is* of science and the *ought* of morality, is a throwback to the Middle Ages, when the church claimed a monopoly on both morality and science and burned people for believing that the earth revolved around the sun as promiscuously as it burned people for believing that Jesus was not the son of God. This way of thinking has been repudiated not only by contemporary science and philosophy but also by virtually all modern religious groups, including the Catholic Church, to which Keyes subscribes. The Catholic Church accepts the scientific findings of evolution but categorically rejects the despicable and immoral belief that "might makes right" or that justice is for the strong alone. Indeed, it opposes abortion as a moral matter while accepting evolution as a scientific truth—a dichotomy Keyes finds hard to accept.

Keyes also argues that without an intelligent creator—in his view, the God of the Bible—there can be no truth, even scientific truth. His non sequitur goes something like this: Truth requires "a kind of intelligent cohesion that could ultimately be known and understood." And if we have "dispensed with the idea of an intelligent creator,"[31] we can have no truth! He confuses, of course, "intelligence" as a source of nature with "intelligible" as a way of understanding nature. We are perfectly capable of understanding—that is, making intelligible— a phenomenon produced without intelligence. Scientists understand the random movement of particles, the division of single-cell organisms, the spasms of unconscious patients, and myriad other physical phenomena. Unless Keyes is relying on the tautology that every phenomenon is the product of an intervening God—a tautology based on faith, not science—he is simply wrong in arguing that without God there can be no scientific truth. There is scientific truth. Only time will tell whether Darwin's theory (or Einstein's or anyone else's) passes the demanding scientific tests of truth. But the existence or nonexistence of God is monumentally irrelevant to this issue of science.

Jefferson, too, was wrong in relying on "the Laws of Nature" for the moral basis of the rights asserted in the Declaration. He thought that he needed a source outside of the law as a trump, and at the time he was writing, natural law was that trump for people who rejected biblical law, as Jefferson did. Indeed, in those days, natural law was seen by more secular radicals, such as Rousseau, Spinoza, and Leibniz, as the progressive alternative to divinely revealed biblical law. Natural law was progressive in several senses: First, it was available to all who could observe nature and did not require Bibles, churches, prophets, priests, or government officials to translate or interpret the revealed word of God; second, its content was not fixed by the dead hand of the past, which all too often justified tyranny, authority, and repression; and third, these progressive proponents of natural law could infuse it with "better" natural rights, as Jefferson did with the right to secede and the rights of life, liberty, and the pursuit of happiness.

But today's more conservative proponents of natural law seek to infuse it with their own repressive values. Read how Alan Keyes uses the natural law of the Declaration of Independence to rail against homosexuality precisely because it may help gay men "pursue happiness":

And so once you have seen in the Declaration the logic that it defined, it is suddenly pretty clear that the first thing you have to remember is that freedom is not an unlimited license, it is not an unlimited choice, it is not even an unlimited opportunity. *Freedom* is, in fact, in the first instance, a responsibility. And it is in the first instance a *responsibility* before the God from whom we come. And now, see, I think that that has—once you start to think it through—tremendous consequences, because it also warns us against that understanding of rights which is based upon radical selfishness. You can't base rights on radical selfishness without asserting that *we are,* ourselves, *the source of those rights.* Once you have denied that, then radical selfishness becomes a contradiction of freedom. And those who then present to us the paradigm of family life, for instance—gay marriage and so forth. And people always say, "Well, what's wrong with that is that I disapprove of homosexuality." No. Let's leave that aside for the moment. I may disapprove of homosexuality. But from the point of view of public policy, what's wrong with it is that it is based upon an understanding of human sexuality that is radically selfish. By definition, I am in this relationship in order to gratify myself. Whereas, what? The foundation of the family is actually an understanding that in that relationship there is a necessary responsibility and obligation which transcends self-gratification in order to connect you with that which is your obligation to the child that may be born of it. You see? And so we can't accept it. Because if we go down that road we are rejecting the responsible understanding of freedom that is implied in the Declaration. [Emphasis added.][32]

Keyes apparently confuses masturbation, which is self-gratification, with homosexuality, which, like heterosexuality, generally involves mutual gratification between partners, and often the responsibility of parenthood. He seems also to be unhappy about mutual gratification not designed for procreation, but even he cannot seriously argue that all harmless pleasures are inherently immoral—as distinguished from amoral—unless they affirmatively serve a noble purpose such as procreation.

To be sure, there are today also advocates of a variation on natural law who seek to infuse it with progressive values. Professor Ronald Dworkin, for example, eschews the phrase "natural law" as too metaphysical. Yet he argues that there are rights that transcend positive law and that can be "discovered" rather than invented. Primary among these rights is that governments must treat all citizens with equal concern and respect. Keyes would probably agree with that broad principle, but Dworkin and Keyes reach precisely the opposite conclusion as to how this equality principle applies to such issues as homosexuality, abortion, capital punishment, teaching evolution and mandating prayer in public schools, and most other agenda-driven disputes in the culture war that divides the Religious Right from the more secular left. In other words, we all agree that equality *should be* a governing consideration; advocates of natural law—from the right and the left alike—think it is a right that can be discovered; I think, however, that it is an important human invention based on our experiences with inequality and that it should be entrenched in the positive law.

Yet, as I have shown, there is little agreement on what this "discovery" or "invention" mandates when it comes to some of the most divisive issues of the day, such as affirmative action or abortion rights. This is not to deny that a consensus regarding equality is important. It is. It marks an important signpost on the road of human development and experience. Based on this consensus, no one who subscribed to the principle of equality could today support slavery, a caste system, overt religious or gender discrimination, and other manifestations of blatant inequality. But that would be true today whether we believed equality came from God, Nature, or human experience. Indeed, those who believe it comes from God or Nature, rather than experience, have a burden to explain why the evils of inequality persisted for so long with the apparent blessing of God and Nature (not to mention the Bible).

If equality—or any other right—came from God or Nature, it would be less subject to evolution than it quite obviously has been. "The Laws of Nature and of Nature's God" are not supposed to change. They are supposed to be immutable. God the Creator does not bungle, and then have to correct His mistakes. But the only thing immutable about laws is that they are always changing, hopefully for the better. The farther away we have gotten from God's revealed law, the better the laws have gotten in regard to slavery, gender inequality, freedom, and justice. The more the laws try to control the evils in human nature (within limits, of course), the better these laws serve a higher morality.

The crowning irony is that some advocates of natural law now cite the Declaration of Independence as positive law, establishing natural law as part of our legal system. The problem, of course, is that even positive law cannot make something out of nothing—or bring into existence something that does not exist. Any attempt to establish natural law through positive law would be like enacting a statute seeking to amend Newton's law of gravity.

What, then, is the source of higher morality if it is not God's revealed word, or "the Laws of Nature and of Nature's God"? It is human experience! Trial and error! We are at our best when we recognize our past mistakes and try to build a better system of morality to avoid repetition of these mistakes! Rights come from wrongs! As Santayana observed, "Those who cannot remember the past are condemned to repeat it." A corollary to that astute observation is that understanding our past mistakes is a prerequisite to avoiding their repetition. Our present system of rights is not based on Nature or God, but rather on a recognition of our past wrongs and a desire not to repeat them—or do worse. We may attribute these ever-changing rights to God or Nature, but unless God changes His mind as often as people do, or unless He learns from His own mistakes, His name—and that of Nature—is being invoked in vain simply to add authority to changes based on human experience and reason.

Although the Declaration is remembered for its opening paragraphs filled with rhetorical flourishes about God-given unalienable *rights*, most of its words are about human *wrongs*. It was the wrongs committed against the colonists by the king, and those representing him, that were the stimuli to secession. It was the British wrongs that inspired the Americans to claim their own rights.

Rights Come from Wrongs

The Declaration's recitation of wrongs began with a general accusation: "The History of the present King of Great-Britain is a History of repeated Injuries and Usurpations, all having in direct Object the Establishment of an absolute Tyranny over these States." It then continues with a bill of particulars in the form of "Facts . . . submitted to a candid World." These facts—many of which were disputed by British lawyers and politicians as well as by some American Tories—were stated in tendentious and somewhat conclusory terms. Historians have disagreed about the validity of particular allegations, but there is widespread agreement that the essence of the complaint was valid: namely, that the colonists were being denied the right to self-determination and self-governance, and that the consequence was a despotism that was anything but benevolent.

What is noteworthy—and enduring—about the catalog of wrongs is how so many of them relate to the rights subsequently enshrined in the Constitution and its first ten amendments. Among the wrongs was denial of trial by jury, lack of an independent judiciary, transfer of defendants to distant places for trial, the quartering of troops during peacetime, and the superiority of military over civil power. All of these wrongs were remedied by constitutional rights—some structural, some particular. What is surprising is that other notorious wrongs that were also addressed in the Constitution—such as general searches and the punishment of dissent—were not included in the Declaration of Independence.

When I argue that rights come from wrongs—as I do in more detail in my 2004 book *Rights from Wrongs* (New York: Basic Books)—I do not mean to suggest that the wrongs themselves inevitably produce rights. If Nazi Germany had won World War II, it is uncertain whether Jews would have had any rights. But Germany lost, and many rights—beginning with the Nuremberg trials—were recognized in reaction to the Nazi wrongs. The relationship between wrongs and rights may perhaps be analogized to that between an infection and the production of antibodies. An infection, like a wrong, often stimulates the production of antibodies that then protect against recurrence. Positive rights are political antibodies to a recurrence of wrongs. Our experience with human wrongs often acts as a stimulus for the recognition and entrenchment of new rights. This process requires human intelligence and an ability to learn from our experiences. The wrongs serve as stimuli to human reason and action. This combination often results in the recognition of new rights or a renewed appreciation and enforcement of old ones.

How Can Conflicting Rights Be Resolved?

Natural law also poses a serious problem when one right comes into conflict with another. If rights come directly from

Nature or Nature's God, as Jefferson believed, how are conflicting claims of rights supposed to be resolved? This was an especially difficult question for deists, who believed in a non-intervening God who reveals his rules through the silent workings of Nature. Even if Nature were to speak, it would speak with a forked tongue. It tells one group of people that it favors a woman's right to choose abortion, and another group of people that it opposes all abortion. It says to some that homosexuality, masturbation, premarital sex, and nonmissionary-position intercourse are all unnatural, while to others that any legal restrictions on consensual adult sex are unnatural. It tells the members of the National Rifle Association that they have the right to bear arms, while it tells supporters of the Brady Bill that they have a right to control and regulate the possession of guns.

A nonintervening God and a silent Nature cannot be expected to answer questions about what they really think of these competing claims of right. Nor did Jefferson and his colleagues trust the words of priests, prophets, or oracles who claim to know God's answer. For Jefferson, the practical resolution of this problem lay in government based on the consent of the governed: "to secure these [unalienable and God-given] Rights, Governments are instituted among Men, deriving their just Powers from the Consent of the Governed." But what if a majority of the governed consent to an action that a minority believes is in violation of "the Laws of Nature and of Nature's God"? What if the governmental institution selected to resolve certain conflicting claims of right—say, the U.S. Supreme Court—resolves it in a way that many believe violates "the Laws of Nature and of Nature's God"? Jefferson's only answer—short of one side persuading the other to change its mind—appears to be physical force, that is, revolution, though not "for light and transient causes." The Declaration states: "whenever any Form of Government becomes destructive of these Ends, it is the Right of the People to alter or to abolish it." If this is the case, then who decides whether a majority of the governed have "become destructive of these Ends"? Who decides whose claim of right prevails? If the answer is the stronger in battle, then might would indeed make right—or at least determine whose "right" prevailed. This is surely a less than satisfying resolution, especially for those who believe in an orderly world in which justice, rather than might, should prevail.

A perfect example of conflicting claims of right—at least to the signers of the Declaration of Independence—revolved around the issue of slavery. Many colonialists believed that the right to own property was natural and God-given, and that African slaves were property. They pointed to the Bible in support of slave ownership and to the "natural" differences between whites and blacks and the "superiority" of the former over the latter. Others believed that all people, including black slaves, were created equal and that slavery was a violation of "the Laws of Nature and of Nature's God." Moreover, a majority of voters—a category that did not include blacks—in most states clearly favored slavery, while an evolving majority in others probably did not.

How then should these conflicts—between different conceptions of natural law and different majorities—be resolved? They were prudentially resolved by postponement, indecision, compromise—and eventually by a U.S. Supreme Court decision (in the *Dred Scott* case) that many believe was in violation of "the Laws of Nature and of Nature's God." This led to the use of force. Might and right turned out to be on the same side in the Civil War, but, sadly, it does not always turn out that way. (I am reminded of a politically incorrect bumper sticker that reads: "War never solved anything—except for ending slavery, Nazism, and genocide.") Had force not been employed, or had the wrong side won, slavery probably would still have been abolished—but much later—as a result of a changing moral consensus based on a recognition of the wrongness of slavery. This recognition grew out of our collective experiences with the evils of that institution: the wrongs of slavery eventually would have led to the right to be free from it. But these wrongs were not "self-evident" to all the signers of the Declaration of Independence, and neither was the right to be free from slavery, as we will see from focusing on the most significant change made in Jefferson's draft by Congress—the striking of the following paragraph from the draft approved by the five-man drafting committee:

He [King George III of Great Britain] has waged cruel war against human nature itself, violating its most sacred right of life & liberty in the persons of a distant people, who never offended him, captivating and carrying them into slavery in another hemisphere, or to incur miserable death in their transportation thither. This piratical warfare, the opprobrium of *infidel* powers, is the warfare of the *Christian* king of Great Britain. Determined to keep open a market where MEN should be bought & sold, he has prostituted his negative for suppressing every legislative attempt to prohibit or to restrain this execrable commerce: and that this assemblage of horrors might want no fact of distinguished die [*sic*], he is now exciting those very people to rise in arms among us, and to purchase that liberty of which *he* also obtruded them; by murdering the people upon whom *he* also obtruded them; thus paying off former crimes committed against the *liberties* of one people, with crimes which he urges them to commit against the *lives* of another. [Emphasis added.][33]

The history and the fate of these remarkable words speak volumes about whether rights come from "the Laws of Nature and of Nature's God" or whether they are largely a product of the very human processes of evaluating differing experiences over time and place, and effectuating political compromises to achieve tolerable consensus.

Conclusion

One conclusion remains clear: the experiment launched by Jefferson and his fellow patriots, separating church from state, has been a resounding success both for churches and for the state—and most important for the citizens. Churches, synagogues, and mosques are thriving throughout America, at a time when many houses of worship, especially churches, are empty throughout Europe. The state remains strong, far stronger than ever anticipated by the founders. Our "godless constitution" has endured longer than any comparable document in history. Our citizens are free to practice any religion or no religion. In the words of an old folk saying, "It ain't broke, so why fix it."

The wall of separation remains standing, despite intense efforts by fundamentalist wall breakers to tear it down. This great wall of America, invisible to the naked eye, yet more powerful than those made of stone, remains in danger because the pressures on its fragile structure are increasing. There are multiple ironies in this danger.

It is no coincidence, in my view, that organized religion is thriving in America and dying in much of Europe. The separation of church and state is good for religion. When church and state merge, natural antagonism that citizens feel toward their government carries over to the church. Moreover, when the state tries to enforce religious practices, enmity is generated. Witness Israel, a country I visit frequently. Because the mechanisms of the state are employed in support of Orthodox Judaism, a sharp division has developed between the Orthodox community and the vast majority of secular Jews. Many secular Jews feel strongly that their freedoms have been impinged, not only by Orthodox Judaism, but by the state as well. Today there is more anti-Orthodox feeling in Israel than in any other part of the world.

If the wall of separation were to crumble in America, the ultimate losers could well be the churches, the synagogues, and the mosques. To be sure, organized religion would benefit *initially* from the support—financial, political, and ideological—of the state. Many religious leaders who are currently strapped for cash see the wall of separation as a barrier to filling their coffers. But in the long run, organized religions would suffer greatly from state involvement in their affairs. The state, by paying the organist, would call the hymn. This would be a tragedy for both religious and secular Americans. Religion, if it remains independent of the state, can serve as a useful check and balance on excesses of government. For example, during the 1920s, eugenics became the rage among scientists, academics, and intellectuals. Thirty states enacted forcible sterilization laws, which resulted in fifty thousand people being surgically sterilized. In 1927 the United States

Supreme Court upheld these laws in a decision by Justice Oliver Wendell Holmes, an atheist, who wrote, "It is better for all the world, if instead of waiting to execute offspring for crime or to let them starve for their imbecility, society can prevent those who are manifestly unfit from continuing their kind." The only dissenting opinion came from a religious Catholic. Churches fought hard against sterilization laws. In this instance, religion was right; government and science were wrong.

In countries where the state controls religion, it is far more difficult for churches to serve as checks upon the excesses of the state. Were the wall of separation to come crumbling down, disbelievers and skeptics would also suffer greatly—at least at the outset. I doubt we would have crusades, inquisitions, or pogroms as in centuries past, but there would be discrimination. Indeed, even today, there is discrimination in practice despite its prohibition under the Constitution. In the long run, however, the number of openly skeptical Americans would increase. Church membership would drop.

Would this be good for America? Would this be good for secular humanists? Since none of us is a prophet, it is impossible to know with certainty what an America without a wall of separation would look like. It would almost certainly become a different place from the one we now inhabit, which is still the envy of the world. We are a prudent and cautious people. As such, we should not take the risks of breaking an edifice that has served us so well for so long.

We must have separation between church and state if we really believe in equality in America—and even equality is an experiment if one considers all the countries of the world today and how few espouse and enforce real equality. Look at Eastern Europe, where in many places the shackles of communism are being exchanged for the shackles of religion.

Some of the same liberal Romanian students who were demonstrating against communism in the streets are now demonstrating for church-sponsored schools and for laws against abortion. In Poland the government has introduced mandatory Catholic education into the public schools, clearly declaring Protestant, Jewish, atheist Poles and others to be second-class citizens.

America is unique. Aside from the Native American population, we are all immigrants. The recency of our arrival on these shores is only a matter of degree, and as the generations pass, our ethnic origins become less important. In its first century of existence, when it was populated largely by white Anglo-Saxons, the United States was only a small country with great aspirations, much like Canada, Australia, New Zealand, and others that have broken free from Britain. We became the greatest country in the world in our second century, *after* immigration, *after* desegregation, *after* women became enfranchised. We became the great America *because* of our diversity, not *despite* our diversity.

Without separation of church and state, it will be difficult for the United States to continue in our status as leader of the free world. Yet the wall of separation gets challenged at every turn, particularly during elections, when politicians not only wrap themselves in the flag but in the cross as well. During the 1984 presidential campaign, Walter Mondale found it necessary to remind Ronald Reagan that in the United States the president, unlike the queen of England, is "not the defender of the faith" but rather the defender of the Constitution. At that point I had written a column that I sent to political candidates across the country setting out what I called "the Ten Command*ments* for Politicians." A Com*mend*ment is something between a commandment and an amendment. They were:

1. Do not claim God as a member of your party or that God is on your side of an issue.

2. Do not publicly proclaim your religious devotion, affiliation, and practices, or attack those of your opponents.

3. Do not denounce those who differ with you about the proper role of religion in public life as antireligious or intolerant of religion.

4. Do not surround your political campaign with religious trappings or symbols.

5. Honor and respect the diversity of this country, recalling that many Americans came to these shores to escape the tyranny of enforced religious uniformity and, more recently, enforced antireligious uniformity.

6. Do not seek the support of religious leaders who impose religious obligations on members of their faith to support or oppose particular candidates.

7. Do not accuse those who reject formal religion of immorality. Recall that some of our nation's greatest leaders did not accept formal or even informal religion.

8. Do not equate morality and religion. Although some great moral teachers were religious, some great moral sinners also acted in the name of religion.

9. When there are political as well as religious dimensions to an issue, focus on the political ones during the campaign.

10. Remember that every belief is in a minority somewhere, and act as if your belief were the least popular.

I wish that instead of the Ten Commandments, the first ten amendments to our Constitution would be put up in schools. Remember that even the most basic issues of separation are not universally accepted in this country. In 1987 Judge W. Brevard Hand of Alabama ruled that each state may establish its own religion, just as it may pick its own bird, flower, song, and motto. Edwin Meese, who was then attorney general, agreed with him. He took out his copy of the Constitution and showed it to a friend of mine who was then at the Justice Department and said, "*Show me* where it says that states cannot establish a religion. All it says is that *Congress* may not establish a religion." And, of course, historically, Hand and Meese were absolutely right—if you stop the Constitution at about the time of the Civil War. The First Amendment of the Constitution was not intended to restrict state establishment of religion, and several states did not establish religions. As late as the middle of the nineteenth century Jews, Turks, infidels, and other non-Christians were precluded from holding office and swearing oaths as witnesses. Catholics, too, did not have full equality during the early period of our nation.

When Hand was asked, "What will people do who have no religion or who belong to a minority religion?" he replied, "A member of a religious minority will simply have to develop a thicker skin if the state establishment offends him." When I saw the statement, I wrote a column in which I gave Hand the "Ayatollah Khomeini Award" for attempting to divide the country along religious lines and described the implications of his view. In Massachusetts, for example, the struggle for official recognition would be between Catholics and Protestants. Where I grew up, in Brooklyn, the religious warfare would be among the Jews. In Utah, Mormonism would prevail; in California, the various cults and fringe religious groups might unite to present a common front. Even if a state settled on Protestantism, which denomination would be the official one? Fortunately the Supreme Court of the United States reversed Judge Hand, characterizing his views as "remarkable," which is a judicial euphemism for "ridiculous." But we are still, even with the United States Supreme Court, seeing some very dangerous trends. The current Supreme Court may not be as protective of the wall of separation as were previous courts.

The trend of *broadening* religion in order to make it more acceptable has now gained momentum. The Supreme Court has upheld the constitutionality of placing a crèche scene in a Christmas display, as long as a sufficient number of plastic reindeer and other accoutrements of secularity are included. In Pittsburgh, Pennsylvania, the city sponsored a Christmas tree, a crèche, and a Hanukkah menorah. Significantly, as the Court described it, the menorah was placed in "the shadow of the Christmas tree." The Court decided that if displays were allowed to include a Christmas tree, they should also allow a Hanukkah menorah. A lot of people in the Jewish community were disarmed by that decision because it gave them standing alongside Christians. But giving special status to religions is only the first step on the short road to tearing down the wall of separation between church and state.

The second step is for the state, once it says religion is to be preferred over nonreligion, to *define* what religion means. You then have to define what is *true* religion and what is *real* religion. I defended Jim Bakker for principled reason relating to that. In imposing his forty-five year sentence, United States District Judge Robert D. Potter of North Carolina said, "We [pointing to himself] who have a *true* religion are offended by those who are charlatans and have a false religion."

It's not the role of a judge in America to distinguish between true and false religions. Judge Potter is a very religious Catholic and belongs to a church whose doctrines often conflict with those of the evangelical movement. The very idea of judges in this country imposing their own religious values on a sentencing process is un-American. And it's intolerable to the continued separation of church and state.

There is another threat to separation that can be characterized as "back-door establishment." What happens is this: When a majority religion like mainstream Christianity seeks state help in promoting its religious doctrines at Christmas, the courts sometimes say, "Christianity really is the majority religion in this country; therefore, when something happens in the name of Christianity, it's really secular, because so many Americans are Christians. Christmas is a secular holiday. But if a smaller religion were to seek aid from the state, since the members are only a minority, then it would clearly be an establishment."

This is *precisely* the opposite of what the framers of our Constitution had in mind. The framers were not fearful of small, fringe, minority religions; they were fearful of the *majority* religion.

The late Chief Justice William Rehnquist expressed this view. In 1986, a chaplain in the air force named Dr. S. Simcha Goldman, who was a psychologist, wore a yarmulke to court when testifying in a case. He was disciplined for violating uniform regulations. The Supreme Court did not uphold his claim of religious observance, because to do so would establish religion. Justice Rehnquist, who worried about the establishment of Orthodox Judaism in America, had no problems about the establishment of Christianity. He also participated in the crèche decision, saying crèches were constitutional on public land. But which poses a greater danger of establishment: Christian crèches on public land or a yarmulke on the head of an individual?

These are some of the problems that persist. Fundamentalism, tragically, is pervasive throughout the world today. These is almost *no* part of the world that is not seeing an increase in fundamentalism—in know-nothingism; in "I don't want to hear, I don't want to think, I don't want to know, tell me what to do, give me marching orders, point me in the right direction and I'll go!" Nor is this rejection of reason limited to the uneducated or the ignorant. It is growing even among some sophisticated people grasping at faith to give meaning to their lives. Jefferson abhorred that approach to life and government. He believed that the Declaration of Independence declared our independence from the domination of clericalism over democracy and from the domination of faith over reason. Those who reject that kind of approach in religion, in politics, in personal life, and in law are always going to have a very difficult struggle ahead of them. They count on the possibility that the extremes within the movements have the seeds for self-destruction. But this is a dangerous approach because we are witnessing the emergence of far more intelligent, far more presentable fundamental movements throughout the world.

Every day is a new struggle for the separation of church and state. We must be willing to buck the tide of majority intolerance and to struggle against religious bigotry because we share Jefferson's vision. We know what losing this battle will do to America. We *know* that the greatness of this country depends on its being the most heterogeneous, the most diverse country in the world. We understand the experimental nature of the American dream.

If Thomas Jefferson could observe our nation today, he would, I believe, be pleased as well as surprised. He would be pleased that the wall he deemed so essential still stands, despite so many challenges and threats. He would be pleased that our complex system of checks and balances—between the branches of government as well as among churches, the media, the academy, the economy, and other nongovernmental institutions—is working. He would be surprised at the increasing power of the federal government, and especially of the executive, and of the relative weakness of the states. He would be surprised, most of all, at how his own views were being hijacked by the Religious Right in an effort to use him as a battering ram against the wall of separation between church and state that was so central to his theory of governance. He would regard this deliberate distortion as a form of civil blasphemy that should be confronted in the marketplace of ideas and soundly rejected.

APPENDIX

The Declaration of Independence

IN CONGRESS, JULY 4, 1776.

A DECLARATION BY THE REPRESENTATIVES OF
THE UNITED STATES OF AMERICA, IN GENERAL
CONGRESS ASSEMBLED

When in the Course of human Events, it becomes necessary
for one People to dissolve the Political Bands which have con-
nected them with another, and to assume among the Powers
of the Earth, the separate and equal Station to which the
Laws of Nature and of Nature's God entitle them, a decent
Respect to the Opinions of Mankind requires that they should
declare the causes which impel them to the Separation.

We hold these truths to be self-evident, that all Men are
created equal, that they are endowed by their Creator with
certain unalienable Rights, that among these are Life, Liberty
and the Pursuit of Happiness—That to secure these Rights,
Governments are instituted among Men, deriving their just
Powers from the Consent of the Governed, that whenever any
Form of Government becomes destructive of these Ends, it is

the Right of the People to alter or to abolish it, and to institute new Government, laying its Foundation on such Principles, and organizing its Powers in such Form, as to them shall seem most likely to effect their Safety and Happiness. Prudence, indeed, will dictate that Governments long established should not be changed for light and transient Causes; and accordingly all Experience hath shewn, that Mankind are more disposed to suffer, while Evils are sufferable, than to right themselves by abolishing the Forms to which they are accustomed. But when a long Train of Abuses and Usurpations, pursuing invariably the same Object, evinces a Design to reduce them under absolute Despotism, it is their Right, it is their Duty, to throw off such Government, and to provide new Guards for their future Security. Such has been the patient Sufferance of these Colonies, and such is now the Necessity which constrains them to alter their former Systems of Government. The History of the present King of Great-Britain is a History of repeated Injuries and Usurpations, all having in direct Object the Establishment of an absolute Tyranny over these States. To prove this, let Facts be submitted to a candid World.

He has refused his Assent to Laws, the most wholesome and necessary for the public Good.

He has forbidden his Governors to pass Laws of immediate and pressing Importance, unless suspended in their Operation till his Assent should be obtained; and when so suspended, he has utterly neglected to attend to them.

He has refused to pass other Laws for the Accommodation of large Districts of people, unless those People would relinquish the Right of Representation in the Legislature, a Right inestimable to them, and formidable to Tyrants only.

He has called together Legislative Bodies at Places unusual, uncomfortable, and distant from the Depository of their Public Records, for the sole Purpose of fatiguing them into Compliance with his Measures.

He has dissolved Representative Houses repeatedly, for opposing with manly Firmness his Invasions on the Rights of the People.

He has refused for a long Time, after such Dissolutions, to cause others to be elected; whereby the Legislative Powers, incapable of Annihilation, have returned to the People at large for their exercise; the State remaining in the mean time exposed to all the Dangers of Invasion from without, and Convulsions within.

He has endeavoured to prevent the Population of these States; for that Purpose obstructing the Laws for Naturalization of Foreigners; refusing to pass others to encourage their Migrations hither, and raising the Conditions of new Appropriations of Lands.

He has obstructed the Administration of Justice, by refusing his Assent to Laws for establishing Judiciary Powers.

He has made Judges dependent on his Will alone, for the Tenure of their Offices, and the Amount and payment of their Salaries.

He has erected a Multitude of new Offices, and sent hither Swarms of Officers to harrass our People, and eat out their Substance.

He has kept among us, in Times of Peace, Standing Armies, without the consent of our Legislatures.

He has affected to render the Military independent of, and superior to the Civil Power.

He has combined with others to subject us to a Jurisdiction foreign to our Constitution, and unacknowledged by our Laws; giving his Assent to their Acts of pretended Legislation:

For quartering large Bodies of Armed Troops among us:

For protecting them, by a mock Trial, from Punishment for any Murders which they should commit on the Inhabitants of these States:

For cutting off our Trade with all Parts of the World:

For imposing Taxes on us without our Consent:

For depriving us, in many Cases, of the Benefits of Trial by Jury:

For transporting us beyond Seas to be tried for pretended Offences:

For abolishing the free System of English Laws in a neighbouring Province, establishing therein an arbitrary Government, and enlarging its Boundaries, so as to render it at once an Example and fit Instrument for introducing the same absolute Rule into these Colonies:

For taking away our Charters, abolishing our most valuable Laws, and altering fundamentally the Forms of our Governments:

For suspending our own Legislatures, and declaring themselves invested with Power to legislate for us in all Cases whatsoever.

He has abdicated Government here, by declaring us out of his Protection and waging War against us.

He has plundered our Seas, ravaged our Coasts, burnt our towns, and destroyed the Lives of our People.

He is, at this Time, transporting large Armies of foreign Mercenaries to complete the works of Death, Desolation, and Tyranny already begun with circumstances of Cruelty and Perfidy, scarcely paralleled in the most barbarous Ages, and totally unworthy the Head of a civilized Nation.

He has constrained our fellow Citizens taken Captive on the high Seas to bear Arms against their Country, to become the Executioners of their friends and Brethren, or to fall themselves by their Hands.

He has excited domestic Insurrections amongst us, and has endeavoured to bring on the Inhabitants of our Frontiers, the merciless Indian Savages, whose known Rule of Warfare, is an undistinguished Destruction, of all Ages, Sexes and Conditions.

In every stage of these Oppressions we have Petitioned for Redress in the most humble Terms: Our repeated Petitions have been answered only by repeated Injury. A Prince, whose Character is thus marked by every act which may define a Tyrant, is unfit to be the Ruler of a free People.

Nor have we been wanting in Attentions to our British Brethren. We have warned them from Time to Time of Attempts by their Legislature to extend an unwarrantable Jurisdiction over us. We have reminded them of the Circumstances of our Emigration and Settlement here. We have appealed to their native Justice and Magnanimity, and we have conjured them by the Ties of our common Kindred to disavow these Usurpations, which, would inevitably interrupt our Connections and Correspondence. They too have been deaf to the Voice of Justice and of Consanguinity. We must, therefore, acquiesce in the Necessity, which denounces our Separation, and hold them, as we hold the rest of Mankind, Enemies in War, in Peace, Friends.

We, therefore, the Representatives of the UNITED STATES OF AMERICA, in General Congress, Assembled, appealing to the Supreme Judge of the World for the Rectitude of our Intentions, do, in the Name, and by Authority of the good People of these Colonies, solemnly Publish and Declare, That these United Colonies are, and of Right ought to be, Free and Independent States; that they are absolved from all Allegiance to the British Crown, and that all political Connection between them and the State of Great-Britain, is and ought to be totally dissolved; and that as Free and Independent

States, they have full Power to levy War, conclude peace, contract Alliances, establish Commerce, and to do all other Acts and Things which Independent States may of right do. And for the support of this declaration, with a firm Reliance on the Protection of Divine Providence, we mutually pledge to each other our lives, our Fortunes, and our sacred Honor.

NOTES

Introduction: Is the United States a Christian Nation?

1. David Barton, *The Myth of the Separation: What Is the Correct Relationship between Church and State? A Revealing Look at What the Founders and Early Courts Really Said* (Aledo, TX: Wallbuilder Press, 2002), p. 218.
2. Ibid, p. 220.
3. Jon Meacham, *American Gospel: God, the Founding Fathers, and the Making of a Nation* (New York: Random House, 2006), pp. 232–233.
4. George F. Will, "God of Our Fathers: Brooke Allen Argues That the Founding Fathers Did Not Establish a Christian Nation," review of *Moral Minority, Our Skeptical Founding Fathers* by Brooke Allen, *New York Times Book Review*, October 22, 2006.
5. Pauline Maier, *American Scripture: Making the Declaration of Independence* (New York: Alfred A. Knopf, 1997), p. 95.
6. *Towne v. Eisner*, 245 U.S. 418, 425 (1918) (Holmes, J.).
7. David McCullough, *John Adams* (New York: Simon & Schuster, 2001), p. 118.
8. Ibid., p. 119.
9. Ibid.
10. Ibid.
11. Ibid., pp. 120–121.
12. Thomas Jefferson, *Letter to Harry Lee*, May 8, 1825, in *The Life and Selected Writings of Thomas Jefferson* (New York: Franklin Library ed., 1982), p. 577.

13. Joseph J. Ellis, "The Enduring Influence of the Declaration," in Joseph J. Ellis and Edward Countryman, *What Did the Declaration Declare?* (Boston: Bedford/St. Martin's, 1999), p. 18.

14. Thomas Jefferson, *Letter to Roger C. Weightman*, June 24, 1826 (New York: Franklin Library ed.), p. 585.

15. A recent book by Harvard historian David Armitage, titled *The Declaration of Independence: A Global History* (Cambridge, MA: Harvard University Press, 2007), documents the continuing influence of our Declaration on other documents of independence throughout the world.

1. The God of the Declaration: Is He the God of Today's Christian Right?

1. *Edwards v. Aguillard*, 482 U.S. 578, 606–607 (1987) (Powell, J., concurring).

2. Brooke Allen, *Moral Minority: Our Skeptical Founding Fathers* (Chicago: Ivan R. Dee, 2006), p. 74.

3. Letter to John Adams, January 24, 1814, in Allen, *Moral Minority*, p. 186.

4. Ibid., p. 28.

5. Jaroslav Pelikan, "Afterword," in Jefferson, *The Jefferson Bible* (Boston: Beacon Press, 1989), p. 157.

6. Thomas Jefferson, "Appendix," in *Reports of Cases Determined in the General Court of Virginia from 1730 to 1740 and from 1768 to 1772* (Charlottesville, VA: F. Carr and Co., 1829), p. 141.

7. Ibid., p. 142.

8. Allen Jayne, *Jefferson's Declaration of Independence: Origins, Philosophy, and Theology* (Lexington: University of Kentucky Press, 1998), p. 16.

9. Ibid., p. 24.

10. Leo Pfeffer, *Church, State, and Freedom* (Boston: Beacon Press, 1967), p. 211.

11. Allen, *Moral Minority*, pp. xiii–xiv.

12. Pauline Maier, *American Scripture: Making the Declaration of Independence* (New York: Alfred A. Knopf, 1997) p. xix.

13. Peter M. Rinaldo, *Atheists, Agnostics, and Deists in America* (Briarcliff Manor, NY: DorPete Press, 2000), p. 27.

14. Jayne, *Jefferson's Declaration of Independence*, p. 40.

15. Thomas Jefferson, *Letter to Peter Carr*, August 10, 1787, in Thomas Jefferson, *The Life and Selected Writings of Thomas Jefferson* (New York: Franklin Library ed.), pp. 350–351.

16. Thomas Jefferson, *An Act for Establishing Religious Freedom*, in Jefferson, *The Life and Selected Writings of Thomas Jefferson*, p. 254.

17. Thomas Jefferson, *Notes on the State of Virginia*, in Jefferson, *The Life and Selected Writings of Thomas Jefferson*, p. 212.
18. Thomas Paine, *The Age of Reason* (New York: Citadel, 1974), p. 186.
19. Willard Sterne Randall, *Thomas Jefferson: A Life* (New York: Henry Holt, 1993), pp. 85–86.
20. Jayne, *Jefferson's Declaration of Independence*, p. 106.
21. Randall, *Thomas Jefferson*, p. 543.
22. Ibid.
23. Ibid.
24. Jayne, *Jefferson's Declaration of Independence*, p. 34.
25. Charles B. Sanford, *The Religious Life of Thomas Jefferson* (Charlottesville: University Press of Virginia, 1984), p. 147.
26. Paine, *The Age of Reason*, p. 157.
27. Ibid., pp. 52–53.
28. Ibid., p. 53.
29. Ibid.
30. Ibid.
31. Ibid., p. 186.
32. Ibid., p. 53.
33. Ibid., pp. 168–169.
34. Ibid., p. 52.
35. Ibid.
36. Ibid.
37. Jayne, *Jefferson's Declaration of Independence*, p. 34.
38. F. Forrester Church, "Introduction," in Jefferson, *The Jefferson Bible: The Life and Morals of Jesus of Nazareth* (Boston: Beacon Press, 1989), p. 28.
39. Ibid., p. 29.
40. Pelikan, "Afterword," in Jefferson, *The Jefferson Bible*, p. 153.
41. Ibid., p. 156.
42. Church, "Introduction," in Jefferson, *The Jefferson Bible*, p. 27.
43. Thomas Jefferson, *Letter to William Short*, October 31, 1819, in Jefferson, *The Life and Selected Writings*, p. 556.
44. Rinaldo, *Atheists, Agnostics, and Deists in America*, p. 7.
45. Jayne, *Jefferson's Declaration of Independence*, p. 135.
46. Jefferson, *Letter to William Short*, October 31, 1819, in Jefferson, *The Life and Selected Writings*, p. 557.
47. Sanford, *The Religious Life*, p. 90.
48. Jon Meacham, *American Gospel: God, the Founding Fathers, and the Making of a Nation* (New York: Random House, 2006), p. 4.
49. Ibid., pp. 89–90.
50. Ibid., p. 145.
51. Ibid., p. 169.

52. Jayne, *Jefferson's Declaration of Independence*, p. 172.
53. Sanford, *The Religious Life*, p. 142.
54. Ibid., p. 144.
55. Church, "Introduction," in Jefferson, *The Jefferson Bible*, p. 5.
56. Ibid., p. 11.
57. Ibid., p. 5.
58. Jayne, *Jefferson's Declaration of Independence*, pp. 137–138.
59. Ibid., p. 141.
60. Thomas Jefferson, *Letter to Benjamin Rush*, April 21, 1803, in Jefferson, *The Life and Selected Writings*, p. 456.
61. Thomas Jefferson, *Letter to Benjamin Rush*, September 23, 1803, in Jefferson, *The Life and Selected Writings*, p. 449.
62. Isaac Kramnick and R. Laurence Moore, *The Godless Constitution: The Case against Religious Correctness* (New York: W. W. Norton, 1991), p. 89.
63. Ibid., p. 92.
64. Meacham, *American Gospel*, p. 104.
65. Ibid., p. 4.
66. Jayne, *Jefferson's Declaration of Independence*, p. 166.
67. Ibid., pp. 166–167.
68. Joseph J. Ellis, *American Sphinx: The Character of Thomas Jefferson* (New York: Alfred A. Knopf, 1997), p. 310.
69. Jayne, *Jefferson's Declaration of Independence*, p. 99.
70. Rinaldo, *Atheists, Agnostics, and Deists in America*, p. 47.
71. Sanford, *The Religious Life*, pp. 1–2.
72. Rinaldo, *Atheists, Agnostics, and Deists in America*, p. 54.
73. Editor's note in Paine, *The Age of Reason*, p. 47.
74. Stephen L. Carter, *The Culture of Disbelief* (New York: Anchor Books, 1994), p. 25.
75. Paine, *The Age of Reason*, p. 50.
76. Ibid., p. 98.
77. Ibid., p. 178.
78. Sanford, *The Religious Life*, p. 157.
79. Ibid., p. 147.
80. Ibid., p. 145.
81. Jayne, *Jefferson's Declaration of Independence*, p. 39.
82. Sanford, *The Religious Life*, p. 165.
83. Jefferson, *Letter to Benjamin Rush*, April 21, 1803, in *Syllabus of an Estimate of the Merit of the Doctrines of Jesus, Compared with Those of Others* (New York: Franklin Library ed.), p. 459.
84. *Babylonian Talmud;* Shabbat 31a.
85. Sanford, *The Religious Life*, p. 127.

86. Jayne, *Jefferson's Declaration of Independence*, p. 26.
87. Rinaldo, *Atheists, Agnostics, and Deists in America*, pp. 20–21.
88. Alan Dershowitz, *Shouting Fire: Civil Liberties in a Turbulent Age* (Boston: Little, Brown, 2002), p. 11.
89. See generally Stephen Jay Gould, *Rocks of Ages: Science and Religion in the Fullness of Life* (New York: Ballantine, 1999).
90. Pelikan, "Afterword," in Jefferson, *The Jefferson Bible*, p. 159.
91. Church, "Introduction," in Jefferson, *The Jefferson Bible*, p. 22.
92. Jefferson, *The Jefferson Bible*, pp. 49–50.
93. Jefferson, *Letter to Benjamin Rush*, April 21, 1803, in Jefferson, *The Life and Selected Writings*, pp. 456–457.
94. Sanford, *The Religious Life*, p. 2.
95. Kramnick and Moore, *The Godless Constitution*, p. 99.
96. Sanford, *The Religious Life*, p. 3.
97. Randall, *Thomas Jefferson*, p. 291.
98. Jayne, *Jefferson's Declaration of Independence*, p. 30.
99. Jefferson, *Notes on the State of Virginia* (New York: Franklin Library ed.), p. 221.
100. Randall, *Thomas Jefferson*, p. 28.
101. Kramnick and Moore, *The Godless Constitution*, p. 98.
102. Ibid.
103. Anti-Defamation League, *The Religious Right: The Assault on Tolerance and Pluralism in America* (1994), pp. 4–6.
104. Sanford, *The Religious Life*, p. 2.
105. Meacham, *American Gospel*, p. 60.
106. Thomas Jefferson, *To a Committee of the Danbury Baptist Association*, January 11, 1802 (New York: Franklin Library ed.), p. 269.
107. Thomas Jefferson, "Appendix," in *Reports of Cases Determined in the General Court of Virginia*, p. 142.
108. Paine, *The Age of Reason*, p. 98.
109. Sanford, *The Religious Life*, p. 147.
110. Jayne, *Jefferson's Declaration of Independence*, p. 63.
111. Ibid., p. 101.
112. Ibid., pp. 149–150.
113. Sanford, *The Religious Life*, p. 26.
114. Jefferson, *Letter to Roger C. Weightman*, June 24, 1826, in Jefferson, *The Life and Selected Writings*, p. 585.
115. Jayne, *Jefferson's Declaration of Independence*, p. 36.
116. Ibid., p. 37.
117. Ibid., p. 174.
118. Ibid., p. 7.
119. Ibid.

120. *Edwards v. Aguillard*, 482 U.S. 578, 606–607 (1987).
121. Pfeffer, *Church, State, and Freedom*, pp. 209–210.
122. Ibid., p. 208.
123. Ibid., p. 211.
124. Ibid., p. 76.
125. Meacham, *American Gospel*, p. 78.
126. Rinaldo, *Atheists, Agnostics, and Deists in America*, pp. 34–36.
127. Edmond S. Morgan, *Benjamin Franklin* (New Haven, CT: Yale University Press, 2002), p. 29.
128. Ibid., p. 19.
129. Ibid.
130. Ibid., p. 21.
131. Meacham, *American Gospel*, p. 8.
132. Rinaldo, *Atheists, Agnostics, and Deists in America*, pp. 40–41.
133. Ibid., p. 48.
134. David McCullough, *John Adams* (New York: Simon & Schuster, 2001), p. 37.
135. Ibid., p. 42.
136. Rinaldo, *Atheists, Agnostics, and Deists in America*, p. 49.
137. John Adams, *Letter to Thomas Jefferson*, May 5, 1816.
138. Adams, *Letter to Thomas Jefferson*, May 19, 1821.
139. Church, "Preface," in Jefferson, *The Jefferson Bible*, p. ix.
140. David McCullough, *John Adams* (New York: Simon & Schuster, 2001), p. 113.
141. Ibid., pp. 113–114.
142. George Dangerfield, *Chancellor Robert R. Livingston of New York (1784–1813)* (New York: Harcourt, Brace, 1960), p. 293.
143. Carl Becker, *The Declaration of Independence* (New York: Vintage, 1958), p. 152.
144. Ibid., p. 171.
145. Maier, *American Scripture*, p. 143.
146. Jefferson, *Letter to Henry Lee*, May 8, 1825, in Jefferson, *The Life and Selected Writings*, p. 577.
147. Jayne, *Jefferson's Declaration of Independence*, p. 116.
148. Sanford, *The Religious Life*, p. 145.
149. Ibid., p. 146.
150. Sanford, *The Religious Life*, p. 155.
151. Pfeffer, *Church, State, and Freedom*, p. 208.
152. Kramnick and Moore, *The Godless Constitution*, p. 29.
153. Ibid., p. 22.
154. Ibid., p. 17.
155. Ibid.

156. Ibid.
157. Ibid.
158. Becker, *The Declaration of Independence*, p. 26.
159. Pfeffer, *Church, State, and Freedom*, pp. 209–210.
160. Meacham, *American Gospel*, pp. 22–23.
161. Carter, *The Culture of Disbelief*, p. 161.
162. Thomas Jefferson, *An Act Establishing Religious Freedom*, in Jefferson, *The Life and Selected Writings*, p. 253.
163. Kramnick and Moore, *The Godless Constitution*, p. 68.
164. Ibid.
165. Jefferson, *Letter to Benjamin Rush*, September 23, 1800, in Jefferson, *The Life and Selected Writings*, p. 449.
166. Kramnick and Moore, *The Godless Constitution*, pp. 95–96.
167. Meacham, *American Gospel*, p. 24.

2. The Christian Right's Strategy to Turn the Declaration into a Baptismal Certificate

1. Jon Meacham, *American Gospel: God, the Founding Fathers, and the Making of a Nation* (New York: Random House, 2006) p. 109.
2. Dennis Prager, "America, Not Keith Ellison, Decides What Book a Congressman Takes His Oath On," Townhall.com, November 28, 2006, www.townhall.com/columnists/DennisPrager/2006/11/28/america,_not_keith_ellison,_decides_what_what_book_a_congressman_takes_his_oath_on (accessed December 19, 2006).
3. Statement available at www.adl.org/PresRele/DiRaB_41/4934_41.htm.
4. Roy Moore, "Muslim Ellison Should Not Sit in Congress," *WorldNet-Daily Exclusive Commentary*, December 13, 2006, www.wnd.com/news/article.asp?ARTICLE_ID=53345 (accessed December 19, 2006).
5. Rachel L. Swarns, "Congressman Criticizes Election of Muslim," *New York Times*, December 21, 2006.
6. David Barton, *The Myth of the Separation,: What Is the Correct Relationship between Church and State? A Revealing Look at What the Founders and Early Courts Really Said* (Aledo, TX: Wallbuilder Press, 2002), p. 218.
7. Meacham, *American Gospel*, p. 72.
8. Jonathan D. Sarna and David G. Dalin, *Religion and State in the American Jewish Experience* (Notre Dame, IN: University of Notre Dame Press, 1997), p. 84.
9. George F. Will, "God of Our Fathers: Brooke Allen Argues That the Founding Fathers Did Not Establish a Christian Nation," review of *Moral Minority, Our Skeptical Founding Fathers* by Brooke Allen, *New York Times Book Review*, October 22, 2006.

10. Brooke Allen, *Moral Minority: Our Skeptical Founding Fathers* (Chicago: Ivan R. Dee, 2006), pp. 173–174.
11. Declaration Curriculum, p. 143.
12. *The Big Story with John Gibson*, Fox News, February 7, 2005. Transcript available at www.foxnews.com/story/0,2933,146760,00.html.
13. Gary Amos and Richard Gardiner, *Never before in History* (Dallas, TX: Haughton Publishing Company, 1998) p. 129.
14. Andre Weisbrod, *America Is Rooted in the Christian Faith*, RaceMatters.org, racematters.org/americarootedinchristianity.htm (accessed August 2, 2006).
15. H.R. 2679, *Public Expression of Religion, Part 2*, Cong. Testimony, 2006 WLNR,10890978, June 23, 2006.
16. "Who Would Confirm an Atheist to the Supreme Court?" *Human Events*, July 15, 2002.
17. Thomas Aquinas College, located in Santa Paula, California, uses a traditional "Great Books" approach to education and was named by one organization as among the "Top 10 Conservative Colleges." Young America's Foundation, accessible at http://media.yaf.org/latest/2005_2006_top_ten.cfm.
18. Meacham, *American Gospel*, p. 120.
19. Tina Kelley, "Talk in Class Turns to God, Setting Off Public Debates on Rights," *New York Times*, December 18, 2006.
20. Kevin Canessa Jr., "Transcript: A Look at What Was Said in KHS Class," *Observer*, November 21, 2006, www.theobserver.com/archives/2006/11-21-06/transcript.shtml.
21. *Hannity & Colmes: Take Back America*, Fox News, December 8, 2004.
22. Alliance Defense Fund, "Declaration of Independence Banned from Classroom," November 23, 2004, accessible at www.alliancedefensefund.org/news/pressrelease.aspx?cid=3218.
23. *Drudge Report*, November 24, 2004, www.drudgereportarchives.com/data/2004/11/24/20041124220000.htm.
24. *The Today Show*, NBC, January 12, 2005. Transcripts accessible at www.net.org/backpage.asp?art=1459.
25. Reuters, November 24, 2004, accessible at www.msnbc.msn.com/id/6578096.
26. *Hannity & Colmes*, Fox News, November 29, 2004.
27. *The O'Reilly Factor*, Fox News, November 26, 2004.
28. George Landrith, "Boy Scouts and Declaration under Attack," OpinionEditorials.com, December 9, 2004, accessible at http://opinioneditorials/guestcontributions/glandrith_20041209.html.
29. Copies of the handouts can be found as part of Williams's complaint filed in District Court, www.eriposte.com/philosophy/fundamentalism/original_ADF_lawsuit.pdf (accessed December 18, 2006).

30. Allen Jayne, *Jefferson's Declaration of Independence* (Lexington: University of Kentucky Press, 1998), p. 34.
31. Thomas Jefferson's letter to Peter Carr, August 10, 1787, accessible at www.stephenjaygould.org/ctrl/jefferson_carr.html.
32. F. Forrester Church, "Foreword," in Thomas Jefferson, *The Jefferson Bible* (Boston: Beacon Press, 1989), p. 28.
33. Jaroslav Pelikan, "Afterword," in Thomas Jefferson, *Jefferson Bible*, p. 157.
34. F. Forrester Church, "Foreword," in Thomas Jefferson, *Jefferson Bible*, p. 15.
35. Allen Jayne, *Jefferson's Declaration of Independence*, p. 34.
36. Williams handout from lawsuit, pp. 66–69.
37. Alan Dershowitz, *America Declares Independence* (Hoboken, NJ: John Wiley & Sons, 2003), pp. 65–70.
38. Thomas Paine, *The Age of Reason*, Part II, Section 14. Excerpts from William Penn's Frame of Government of Pennsylvania (1682).
39. Ibid, Section 21.
40. Williams handout, p. 21. Exhibit B of Williams's complaint.
41. Williams's citation for the excerpts is William J. Johnson, *George Washington, the Christian* (New York: Abingdon, 1919), pp. 24–35.
42.   O most Glorious God, in Jesus Christ my merciful and loving father, I acknowledge and confess my guilt, in the weak and imperfect performance of the duties of this day. I have called on thee for pardon and forgiveness of sins, but so coldly and carelessly, that my prayers are become my sin and stand in need of pardon. I have heard thy holy word, but with such deadness of spirit that I have been an unprofitable and forgetful hearer, so that, O Lord, tho' I have done thy work, yet it hath been so negligently that I may rather expect a curse than a blessing from thee. But, O God, who art rich in mercy and plenteous in redemption, mark not, I beseech thee, what I have done amiss; remember that i am but dust, and remit my transgressions, negligences & ignorances, and cover them all with the absolute obedience of thy dear Son, that those sacrifices which I have offered may be accepted by thee, in and for the sacrifice of Jesus Christ offered upon the cross for me; for his sake, ease me of the burden of my sins, and give me grace that by the call of the Gospel I may rise from the slumber of sin into the newness of life. Let me live according to those holy rules which thou hast this day prescribed in thy holy word; make me to know what is acceptable in thy holy word; make me to know what is acceptable in thy sight, and therein to delight, open the eyes of my understanding, and help me thoroughly to examine myself concerning my knowledge, faith and repentance, increase my faith, and direct me to the true object Jesus Christ the way, the

truth and the life, bless O Lord, all the people of this land, from the highest to the lowest, particularly those whom thou has appointed to rule over us in church & state. Continue thy goodness to me this night. These weak petitions I humbly implore thee to hear accept and ans. for the sake of thy Dear Son Jesus Christ our Lord, Amen.

43. Ibid.
44. Ibid.
45. Ibid.
46. In this instance, the handout has excerpts from state constitutions. This one was an excerpt from North Carolina's. The handout also included the following quotations (most brackets, ellipses, and quotation marks were in the original handout except the bracketed ellipses):

> Maryland; Article XXXII (1776) ". . . All persons, professing the Christian religion, are equally entitled to protection of their religious liberty . . . the Legislature may, in their discretion, lay a general tax and equal tax, for the support of the Christian religion." [. . .]

Maryland; Article XXXV (1776) "That no other test or qualification ought to be required . . . than such oath of support and fidelity to this State . . . and a declaration of a belief in the Christian religion." [. . .]

Massachusetts; Chapter VI, Article I (1780) "[All persons elected to State office or to the Legislature must] make and subscribe the following declaration, viz.

'I, ____, do declare, that I believe the Christian religion, and have firm persuasion of its truth . . .'" [. . .]

New Jersey; Article XIX (1776) ". . . no Protestant inhabitant of this Colony shall be denied the enjoyment of any civil right . . .; all persons, professing a belief in the faith of any Protestant sect . . . shall be capable of being elected into any office of profit or trust, or being a member of either branch of the Legislature." [. . .]

South Carolina; Article III (1778) "[State officers and privy council to be] all of the Protestant religion." [. . .]

South Carolina; Article XII (1778) ". . . no person shall be eligible to a seat in the said senate unless he be of the Protestant religion."[. . .]

South Carolina; Article XXXVIII (1778) "That all persons and religious societies who acknowledge that there is one God, and a future state of rewards and punishments, and that God is publicly to be worshipped, shall be freely tolerated. The Christian Protestant religion shall be deemed . . . to be the established religion of the state."[. . .]

Vermont; Declaration of Rights, III (1777) ". . . nor can any man who professes the protestant religion, be justly deprived or abridged of any civil right, as a citizen, on account of his religious sentiment . . .; nevertheless, every sect or denomination of people ought to observe the Sabbath, or the Lord's day. . . . "

Vermont; Frame of Government, Section 9 (1777) "And each member [of the legislature], . . . shall make and subscribe the following declaration, viz.:

'I do believe in one god, the Creator and Governor of the universe, the rewarder of the good and punisher of the wicked. And I do acknowledge the scriptures of the old and new testament to be given by divine inspiration, and own and profess the protestant religion.'"

He also distributed colonial laws that required the following oath: "I, ____, do profess faith in God the Father, and in Jesus Christ His only Son, and in the Holy Ghost, one God, blessed for evermore; and I do acknowledge the holy scriptures of the Old and New Testament to be given by divine inspiration."

47. U.S. Constitution, Article VI.

48. From the Williams handout, with excerpts from Jean-Jacques Burlamaqui, *The Principles of Natural Law,* translated by Mr. Nugent (London: J. Nourse, 1748).

49. Settlement for *Williams v. Vidmar,* accessible at www.stevenscreekparents.org/settlement.pdf.

50. In addition to invoking the Nazis as an analogy to nearly every critic of his extreme views, Pat Robertson has himself used language to characterize his opponents that is disturbingly close to the language used by the Nazis to characterize Jews.

"[T]ermites don't build things, and the great builders of our nation almost to a man have been Christians, because Christians have the desire to build something. . . . The people who have come into [our] institutions [today] are primarily termites. They are into destroying institutions that have been built by Christians. . . . The termites are in charge now, and . . . the time has arrived for a godly fumigation."

Compare that to this criticism of Jews by German propagandists: "[Jews are] the eternal parasite . . . that like a horrible bacillus spreads more and more."

In his book *The New Millennium,* Robertson specifically accuses liberal Jews of an "ongoing attempt to undermine the public strength of Christianity" by removing Christian prayers from public schools, and he warned that "sooner or later there would be a Christian backlash of major proportions."

51. The quotations in the text are from Anti-Defamation League, *The Religious Right: The Assault on Tolerance and Pluralism in America* (1994), pp. 6, 12–13. See also Sydney H. Schanberg, "New York; Thoughts of an Infidel," *New York Times*, September 8, 1984, p. 21; Alan Dershowitz, *The Vanishing American Jew* (New York: Little Brown, 1997), ch. 4.

52. Mark DeWolfe Howe, *The Garden and the Wilderness* (Chicago: University of Chicago Press, 1965), p. 6.

53. Gustav Niebuhr, "Religion Journal; Campus Skeptics Unite against Aggressive Faith," *New York Times*, September 28, 1996, p. 12.

54. Garry Wills, *Under God: Religion and American Politics* (New York: Simon & Schuster, 1990), p. 25.

55. ADL, *The Religious Right*, p. 4.

56. *Church of the Holy Trinity v. United States*, 143 U.S. 457, 471 (1892).

57. Ibid.

58. Ibid. at 471 (citing *People v. Ruggles*, 8 Johns, 290, 295 (1811).

59. Dennis Prager, "Judeo-Christian Values, Part 24: Who Believes in American Exceptionalism?" WorldNetDaily.com, November 1, 2005, accessed on February 16, 2007, at www.worldnetdaily.com/news/article.asp?ARTICLE_ID=47157.

60. Barton, *Myth of the Separation*, p. 116.

61. Florida Congresswoman (and Republican Senate candidate) Katherine Harris, in an interview with the *Florida Baptist Witness*.

62. Jake Tapper, "Too Jewish?: Americans Made *Seinfeld* One of the Most popular TV Shows Ever, but Are They Ready to Put a Jew in the White House?" Salon.com, August 9, 2000.

63. Alan M. Dershowitz, "Commentary; Bush Starts Off by Defying the Constitution," *Los Angeles Times*, January 24, 2001.

64. Tony Perry, "Bush Signs Bill to Save San Diego Cross," *Los Angeles Times*, August 15, 2006, p. B1.

65. Judy Holland, "Congressional Conservatives Want to Lift Chaplain Limits," *Houston Chronicle*, September 24, 2006, p. A19.

66. Neela Banerjee, "Proposal on Military Chaplains and Prayer Holds Up Bill," *New York Times*, September 19, 2006, p. A1.

67. "Fighting about Praying," *Los Angeles Times*, October 5, 2006, p. 12.

68. Peter S. Canellos, Michael Kranish, and Farah Stockman, "Bush Brings Faith to Foreign Aid: As Funding Rises, Christian Groups Deliver Help—with a Message," *Boston Sunday Globe*, October 8, 2006, p. A1.

69. Canellos et al., "Bush Brings Faith to Foreign Aid," p. A22.

70. Ibid.

71. Ibid.

72. Ibid.
73. Ibid.
74. Amy Sullivan, "Mitt Romney's Evangelical Problem," *Washington Monthly*, September 2005.
75. "Mitt Romney's Problem," *Economist*, Lexington, September 28, 2006.
76. Barton, *Myth of the Separation*, p. 136.
77. George F. Will, *New York Times*, October 22, 2006.
78. Article 11, Treaty of Peace and Friendship between the United States and the Bey and Subjects of Tripoli of Barbary, passed by 5th Conress in 1797.

3. What Are "the Laws of Nature and of Nature's God"?

1. Allen Jayne, *Jefferson's Declaration of Independence: Origins, Philosophy, and Thought* (Lexington: University of Kentucky Press, 1998), p. 116.
2. Jefferson, *Letter to Peter Carr*, August 10, 1787, in *The Life and Selected Writings of Thomas Jefferson* (New York: Franklin Library ed., 1982), p. 349.
3. Jayne, *Jefferson's Declaration of Independence*, p. 117.
4. Ibid., p. 116.
5. Garry Wills, *Inventing America* (New York: Vintage, 1978), p. 204.
6. Carl Becker, *The Declaration of Independence* (New York, Vintage, 1958), p. 277.
7. A recent book by Harvard Professor Marc D. Hauser, *Moral Minds: How Nature Designed Our Universal Sense of Right and Wrong* (New York: Ecco, 2006) argues that humans have evolved a universal moral instinct and that experience "tunes up our moral actions." Much work remains to be done on these questions.
8. Ronald Dworkin, *Taking Rights Seriously* (Cambridge, MA: Harvard University Press, 1978), p. 158.
9. Ibid., p. 272.
10. Quoted in Alan Dershowitz, *Shouting Fire: Civil Liberties in a Turbulent Age* (Boston: Little, Brown, 2002), p. 56.
11. Ibid.
12. Ibid.
13. Dworkin, *Taking Rights Seriously*, pp. 190–191, 269.
14. Joseph J. Ellis, "The Enduring Influence of the Declaration," in Joseph J. Ellis and Edward Countryman, *What Did the Declaration Declare?* (Boston: Bedford St. Martins, 1999), p. 16.
15. Jefferson, *An Act for Establishing Religious Freedom* in Jefferson *The Life and Selected Writings*, p. 254.

16. Dworkin, *Taking Rights Seriously*, p. 266.
17. Ibid., p. 267.
18. Ibid.
19. Jefferson, *An Act for Establishing Religious Freedom*, in Jefferson *The Life and Selected Writings*, pp. 254–255.
20. Ibid.
21. Ibid., p. 255.
22. Michael Paulson, "Catholics Reject Evangelization of Jews," *Boston Globe*, August 13, 2002.
23. *Bradwell v. State*, 83 U.S. 130 (prior history).
24. *Bradwell v. State*, 83 U.S. 130, 141 (Bradley, J., concurring).
25. Dershowitz, *Shouting Fire*, p. 10.
26. Ibid., p. 495.
27. Jeff Cohen and Norman Solomon, "Cosmo's Deadly Advice to Women about AIDS," *Seattle Times*, July 31, 1993.
28. Alan Keyes, address to the Declaration Foundation, *Declaration Principles Reborn*, August 11, 1996.
29. Keyes, Virginia high school appearance, February 28, 2000.
30. Ibid.
31. Ibid.
32. Keyes, address to the Declaration Foundation, 1996.
33. Becker, *The Declaration of Independence*, pp. 212–213.

INDEX